# The Woman at the Well

ISBN-13 Paperback        978-1-970309-82-9
            eBook        978-1-970309-81-2

Library of Congress Control Number: 2026906452

# The Woman at the Well

## ABIGAIL HAWKINS

H I THIS IS MY STORY my name is Elisa Whitehead, I am 54 years of age, currently a wife and mother of 3 children and 5 step children. This is my third marriage. I live in a little town in Belleville, MI, been only here 7 year. I was born to Willie and Pandora Drake whom they had 12 children. Both parents are gone home to be with the lord. I have 8 siblings who are still alive and that make me the 9th. I have one daughter and two sons Missy Man and Chris. My husband's name is Joaquin. Both of his parents of are *alive* and he has five children and we together have 25 grandchildren and I have the most, but will get into that when we get into the book.

Ok I was born in 1960 in Cleveland, Ohio. I am the 10th child on my mother's side and 7th on my dad's side, which means my mother had 3 children before she married my father. I can go back as far as 2 years old when we live in apartment and three children were still on the bottle. I remember my father getting up to go to work when it was still dark outside and we awaken early along with them crying for bottles. I do not know why but by the time

I was four I was independent and you can say if there ever was a black shrilly temple I fitted the script I can remember crossing the streets and going to the store by myself. I knew what money was and I knew where to get cookies and candy from. My mother was the mother that had so many children she did not know what to do just joking. I remember going to the store without any clothes on and father coming down the street in car from work and saw me and grab me. Me ha I was on my way to the candy store. We would find money in old pocket books that is what we called purses today ha. This was a corner house on the main streets. I remember that all the relatives and the neighbors would be at our house and I did not like that. I did not feel that they had a right to be there I would literally cry and tell them to go home. Wow I was spoiled rotten. My mom would often offer to pay other to help with chores and if they were not our family I would cry and tell her not to give them that dime or quarter or whatever.

Listen at 4 years of age I would get allowance and keep that shiny quarter and keep it save it and would not let anyone exchange it I would know and have a fit if they try to replace the original. Look I was very particular. I have a brother that is a year younger than me but somehow of another he never got a chance to be the baby, I had the spot. Spoil rotten I tell you! For some reason the house was full but it seem like I was my father's only child. I never seen or remember he'll hold touching or playing with the other children but only me. On his off days I was his shadow. They say she is just like Willie and his mother meaning my grandmother. I am trying to get off this year of me being 4 but so much happen in that house. So much was going on the 60's the Beatles the temptations of my father who was a young James Brown at least he wore his hair like him. Listen they had bible and prayer meeting on wed night gambling and party on Friday and Saturday and in church on Sunday. My mother, sister and her two children lived there. My aunt Vie and oldest sister Mae Jean was going with my dad's friends that came over from the church. Oh I forgot to mention my father had a singing group dress like the temptations and act like them but they sang gospel music, but fought the same demons that the world fought. Wow let me not forget playing the numbers my mom and dad play every day and would hit the number enough to buy new cars and whenever we moved, it was because she hit the number.

Now fast forward to 5 years old we move on 105th and Saint Claire wow above a corner bar. Now at this time the other grown kids and relatives move out and it was just us 9 all the kids, my mother and father had together. Wow daddy and momma was never home he work 2 and she work 2 jobs and my sister the first born child of my parents became my mother as a caregiver. Our house was in disarray we know now but not then that you cannot let your 12 years take the place of an adult but my folks were from the countryside and brought the country up north with them. Boy she was liking boys and boys was liking her. We all were stair steps so nobody was in total submission to her but us little ones. Now to my sibling that got another point of view I say to y'all write your own book.

Now moving on wow you talking about action packed times where do we begin. The school yard was directly across the street from us. My brothers joined a gang called the devil disciples yeah you see not good at all. So they were gang fighting and running the streets mind you both parents are working their fingers to the bones. My sister is in love and her boyfriend is over their daily and my other two sisters is trying to be like my older sister and we got a mess call it what you want but yet there was a strong family bond between all of us but everybody was in a mode of representing the family name and at that time it was like making a name and gaining territory. And this was how it was parents came home and did not have a clue who and what they children was or became until reality slap them in the face when the sins of the children could no longer be compress or hidden.

My dad up butt and all in the household fear him from my mother to the uncles cousins you name it he stood ten feet tall...now you may say if they or y'all feared him why was you all disobedience, well my only answer is foolishness on the kids part not knowing then that your sins will find you out.

But when the straw broke the camel back, when my 12 or 11 year old brother was shot over 12 times in an arm robbery and it was all over the news. They broke into a drug store and were caught and cops shot him over 12 times and that was a turning point for us all. I remember him coming home and we all seeing the bullets holes in him I no more than 6 or younger wow. I remember during those times we would all lay on the floor and watch Batman and Robin outer limits out of space and our regular snacks was Kool aid and cookies and baloney sandwich and mayonnaise or mustard sandwiches wow we love it. Back then one cent could get you three cookies 5 cents Sherbet and 10 cents soda under 10cents 5 cents chips.

Across the streets the store sold chicken feet and we bought it like crazy. In those days stores would set fruits outdoors in front of the store we knew how to steal some. Days when we were hungry and take fruit sometimes not often but sometimes we did. I went to the community recreation center and won a dance contest off the record going to the Smokey Robinson hit song. The Supremes was the hottest group. Ok getting back to the story but it cannot forget the we play hop scotch and jump rope and jacks and that is what we did day in and out and when the sun went down rock teacher and what time is it Mr. Foxx. Now after my brother got shot it was time to move to 115 Sinclair. Now were back in a single home on a street where there is homeowner and a tight nit neighborhood meaning all or everyone knew each other. My parents were still working, and my sister is 15 or 16 now she discovered herself and everyone is pretty going finding themselves. I am in the first grade now then I mentioned I had very low self-esteem outside from home.

Children in kindergarten mess me up they were so mean they would not touch me hold my hand when we were to hold hands. It was a terrible experience day in and day out, I did not like school at all. At that age I discover the emotion, shame and I was ashamed of many things from that point on. Well my first grade class was great, my teacher was white and a hippy she was young and she did not see color, well my 11 month older sister had her before me. And her name was Ms. Slavery she wore her hair parted down the middle she was just cool.

We stayed after school and help her, she brought us home. We were in plays and it was fun time. Oh the bug got on me I was so fast I fell in love with Michaels Martin My friend Cathy likes Robert and we were two women when we step in our class because we had boyfriends. Wow I call him on the phone can you imagine at 6 calling a boy well I did and did it regularly. My mother had her first child at 13 and down south they were married with 2 at 13. Her daughters had the bug bad. Wow you know it is crazy but as mess up as the family but it was the best family. Out of all the crazy and sick things that happened I never once wish I had a different mother or father or sibling I always felt like I had the best even though I often was ashamed mostly because of others view of them, my view was they were the greatest. See there I go again very protective. Ok. My mom got pregnant now have a baby again now I am seven going on 17 it is in the blood and I have a younger brother a year younger.

At this point my dad's relationship with me is still tight and he spoiling me rotten. But everybody thought I was going to trip cause of my little birth but truth be told I was very excited of her arrival but the rumor was so embedded that they really wanted me to lose that seat of being the baby because everyone was jealous of our relationship and they showed it. Oh so horrible how my sisters treated me all my life growing up they kept me away and punish me by not allowing me to be part of the group I was often told you cannot come in my room and all sibling will be in the room but me it was the norm. Well my sister that was next to me but older really did not like the way they treated me and would come with me, we were like twins people thought we were. Honestly we were the closest then and now of all the siblings.

I started to like my life. The house is downsizing the oldest sister got pregnant had a child one month 2 days after my mother had my sister. In and out but mostly out the next in line sibling could not wait to get the position. The gang bangs brothers they are now living the fast lane, one is a Bonnie and Clyde character to the tee and the other in jail. Three gone wow I remember being ashamed because my mother had 12 kids and kids would make fun of that even though there were large family back then. But father had a nervous breakdown working three jobs and the family covers it up. I remember seeing my grandmother his mom for the first time. It was amazing I had never seen silver hair before and she was from another world she chewed tobaccos and dip snuff and spit in the can wow. Really I am trying to write an overview without getting into other folk business because the books suppose to be about me but I am writing about us.

Seven siblings in the house, I can start raise my head up. Now the oldest in the lead is 12 and my sister Lilac, while she is different she is into fashion exploring and it seems like she got favorite with mom and dad cause she's asking things the other sibling did cracked they lips to ask. Wow I got a new mom and dad because they are not the same parents they were when the other three were with us. This is called softening breaking down. So now we're breathing as a family with the other older siblings being a shadow in sense they have a lot of issues and problems but their aunt feasting in our house and that was all that matter. Beside old Willie had a loud roar and when they could not suppress they're behavior they had to go or would not dare bring it to the house and mama got smart and quit covering for them and started hiding behind her husband when she did not want to deliver their request.

Oh did I mention on 115 we went to park Jazz festivals and we would go to the YMCA for recreation. Only eight and nine we had purple bikes we would go everywhere wow God was with us we road miles when our parents were at work. Oh the corner store we would have to go get lunch I never forget the grocery clerk in meat department wore white lab coats and wrap your meat in paper then sealed it with a rubber band and they weight all your meats. Did I tell you that the milk man use to deliver milk to our hues in a glass bottle that was some good milk? Now when my parents came home we all ate dinner at the table everyone had to come to the table no matter what went on. We set our table and when mom reduce the work schedule dinner was cook daily.

Holidays was the best, my father barbequed every holiday and my mom did the sides and never did we not pack the food up and head to the park for family picnic. Daddy would meet with his buddies from church and you would not know that they were a gospel group and would be drinking and baseball was their game. Me and my sister every year would have our picnic boyfriends and that we only see only at the picnic. Shame shame shame. By this time daddy is drunk or high whatever you want to call it and a fight would break out just about every holiday. It's about driving too fast and the kids are scared in the car. I never forget lest back track back on Melrose when I was 4 and 3 a fight broke out between dad and mama on a Saturday afternoon don't know till this day what it was about. But daddy had mama and he was wiping her she grab that pretty hair of hers. He jot got done at the Barbara shop all wavy shining and pretty and she grabbed his hair and wrap it around her wrist as many times as it would go and he got off her cause he was so concern about his pretty hair she let him go and he did not put his hands back on her cause he was so concern about his hair and making it back to the Barbara so they can fix it. He use to walk me and put me on his shoulder I never forget he brought me over my mother's friend house, I thought that was strange but it was what it was. I remember he and I were not supposed to be there. I believe the Lord would tell him do not bring this child over this women house again.

At 5 pardon me people but remembering summer day leaving the park on a holiday. He was drunk about ten kids were in the car sitting on the floor everywhere. They fussing the whole drive back because when he's drunk he like to drive fast. We make home stop at the Clark gas station they begin to fight I guess my mild manner mother said not today brother. She balled her fence and sock him in the nose so hard she left him alone and let the liquor wear off. Well next chapter we pack our bags and move 23 miles from the city.

My mother had had it with her sons living a life of crime and watching the girls making wrong hurtful choices in their life. My sister who was12 turn 13, her boyfriend died from poisons so much stuff. It seems as though we were living Motown sounds in every way, neighbor died from playing Russian roulette. So went out from that small town, 23 miles outside from the city wow this was the best thing my parents did for us because this move impacted my life and carried us where we are today.

Wickliffe Ohio yeah 2 or 3% black wow it seem like we died and all went to heaven. We rented the house a white man I think Sheldon was his name. Nice community there was four streets of blacks in the entire city. Italians we call them dagos Greeks white polish wow what a community school buses beautiful schools. Wow order discipline football teams pepper rallies tennis. The land was rich we had in our yard grape vines cherry tree apple pear trees. At the corner plum and peach trees tastier than Georgas groves. Horse at our playground full basket ball courts. The still quietness of the night. Even the skunks I liked the smell it did not bother me. Just pure beauty. Taking lunch to schools you see we did not have that in the city schools. No crimes no foolishness ever did see my brothers hardly during that time cause they were criminals and they did not want to be hassle by the cops. yeah peace for my parents.wow finally I feel like somebody out there you did not have to prove yourself the fact that you made it there and live there you were automatically there and protected by the government of the community. Third grade I was and quickly 4th grade now there lilac was in senior high daisy in the 6 unique 5 me in the 4 mike in the 3rd and trice still a baby. Daddy down to one job and mama one job. A family order no overseer dad and mom in the rightful place. They had three sets of kid's age group and each group was night and day so different. Well you know the 70's came and it was party time this community work and play they believe in community and fellowship in a positive way, no foolishness to it. There was a party every weekend among the youth not the parents at least not mines. Wow from nine to 10 I liked Michael foster but when t turned 11 it was Titus Taylor all the way.

My friends were cheerleader and sports players. In school we was taught home economics we took gym three times a week we bake sewing class. We took French every year by the time I got to the seven grades I could speak it. Woo wow turning point learning so much and wow it only last 4 years and our house burn down and back to the city we came. Now let me tell you why that happens, oh and I will be going back and forth as I remember. My brother came to visit he had not been out there very long. My father brother was robbed and was in a comma=a family came to our house to give us support nothing had never happen like this in our family. While waiting for him to come out the comma my cousin at the house decide to and walk to the store mind you the store was far away on route to the store you pass a funeral home so in passing my relative decide to go in and low in behold there is an envelope sitting on the register podium he see it and take it and pursue to go to the store now he is with my sister Niue she 11 at the time he is 20 or over the open and it is someone funeral home money he tell her not to tell and buys everyone goodies. This stays a secret. A wee uncle dies and lasted our house burns to the ground. More to the story he brought a curse to the house to take money of someone when long story short his action of evil brought a curse on our household. From that point on things went down in our family you can say like a dark cloud following us. The house burn down and we was force to move back to the city. When we moved back to the city it was not welcome on my part. So much shame and humiliation being a victim of a house fires and losing everything. Having to be in hotels and get handouts watching your parent's expression of fear and despair not knowing what to do. I remember waiting on the place to open for us to move in we stayed with the relative that stole the funeral home money isn't that ironic. and yes all sorts of things was going on and happening there but we said not a word and suddenly that place that we were waiting on looked very appealing to me almost as good as the place we left that burn down. well finally into our new place and our new community the home was good and the community ok but the reality of where we were planted now was seen through the school system. Rioting in the class room dysfunctional behavior everywhere I look I said no this cannot be. The bullying and the intimidation were so relevant. I thought really I was frightened every day I walk in and near the school. I force into going along and getting involved in their activities by the bad girls the gang girls. Only God protected I have never cut school before and here I found myself cutting school misplace in a house were Satan rule right at the corner of our street. It was if they the people put a watch out for the innocent to grab them and recruit them to be a product of evil activity. I remember I felt as if I was being sold to evils fighting over me. One boy she will be mine and another no she will be mine. So because of the confusion and the distractions I was put on hold and was able to escape the auction lol. We one fellow that was in the behind scenes decided he would get me meaning take me for his girlfriend because I was fresh new and to him from a different world. Now here is where the story begins. Randy calls me and insist that I become his girlfriend and I first was not interest but his pressuring me broke me down, and I became attracted to his persistence. Long story short we began dating and while we start dating I begin to discover that he had a reputation in the neighborhoods with the girls beyond belief and this holding onto him cause me to experience and face challenges I was not mature enough to endure. I became engrafted into the life of the community. Oh did I tell you I was 13 and 16 when all this began. This young boy wore a derby hat and velvet blazer jacket and he walk with a cane stick not because he was cripple but. But that was the cool thing to do at that time. he did not go to school he shot dice and play cards and when he did honest work he would go with his granddad and do handy man small jobs and this is what I was capture by. Well during this time we dated and I was a virgin for two years into our dating. He would be with others girls I knew but because I was not ready he presume others I knew. But in my eyes I took it that he honored me. Well the summer of 1974 I went on a family vacation to Mississippi to visit relatives and meeting cousins I had never met before I decided to stay. And down south I chop cotton and experience many things. I had a great time and, I remember calling home and my parents let randy speak to me on the phone I thought what is randy doing there and we are sneaking dating because my dad doesn't allow boyfriends, but I said wow huh this is different he said he miss me and I told him the same you see

I was down there for the summer and school was starting back and I needed to get home.

So getting home I was happy eager to get home I had never been away from home before for that length of time. I will never forget the turning point of my life when I was mostly a typical girl and obedient to my parents, immediately things changed in that area. I was freshly home and my boyfriend whom I married down the line were in our basement and we were kissing and touching but was not going beyond that and I remember my sister who was 2year older than I was uncomfortable of our actions of kissing but I did not know that I somehow that that I was her equal since she had a child at 16. But me being very naive I did not know that because I was her sister even though she indulged she did not want her younger sister to. so she told my dad that I had had company and that it was a boy and that we were probable doing grown up things, well I was confronted and I told my dad that we were not doing the things that she said we were and my father believe her. Later on I heard him say to my mom that she will be pregnant before or after she turn 16. Well that hurtled my feeling because I thought I was being good keeping my virginity from my boyfriend who was very sexual active. But being a Christian knows and my belief I know that was wrong to allow any one touch my body in the way that I allowed that you are not married to. So the next time randy appeal to me I told him yes they believe that I am having sex anyhow so why not. I remember disrespecting my parents home and allowing him to have me as often as he desire. Well I was safe for about a year without getting pregnant. But I was so disconnect. I had moved my relationship from my dad and became removed from the family in more ways than one. Reflecting back on that time I was so unhappy. I did not like what I had got myself in to my life I had given it to randy. Our relationship became violent I was in abusive relationship. And I did what most victims does I kept it secret and protected my abuser. well it was moving time again we had been there almost 4 years not quite to and upscale community not as far away but the outskirts of the community. Well this was my brake I thought to get a new life second chance he will not have access to me because he does not drive. Oh let me tell you a little about his background. He was raise by his mother she was adopted and she had him when she was 14. His father rejected them and abandon them and went off to the army his mom had another child at 16 and both fathers abandon his mother. So when I came in the picture sneaking and doing what I had no business doing his mama was 31 or 32 years of age with a grandbaby because his sister had a child at 14. So he had no positive male role models in his life that I seen but his adopted granddad that I feel he respected him but was determined that he was going to live his life the way he wanted to. Well yes he seen his mom get beat and be on the system the welfare. So he became a product of his environment an easy way to some things up. So back to the new neighborhood it was a good move on my parent's parts and we had all the benefits of the neighborhood we left when we got burn out. Oh when that happen I was 12. I remember having a conversation with randy concerning me moving away and he said oh so this is the end of our relationship right and of course I said no we will continue someway and then he flip and said you all are moving to that nice community people like me are not good enough to come there I know you will find a boyfriend from there. And suddenly I said no I will not leave you knowing it was a possibility. But he had me say that I will not leave him and I felt bonded by my words. So the move came and I had a breather from him and life was bestowed to me and I start plans for my life and this was 1976 the summer. My dad had been faithful in his continuance of attending church services and he would go out of town quite regular because he was the booking manager of his gospel group. So this particular summer July of 76 he was on his way out of town and my sibling decided to have a party we he leaves. Because they was proud of our new home and our beautiful house. So this was show off time. now on the party list randy gets wind of it and shows up and I did not want him there but the victim mentality came on me as if it never left and when he showed up we pick up where we left off. Not proud to say but I allowed him to have me in my parents' home were no defilement had taken place until that time. I remember thinking let this over and when I get free from this I will make sure that I for real go my way he his way. Well that time was over and I got busy working with my mom at the holiday inn hotel my sister and I. I thought we had died and went to heaven our whole surrounding was good no financial lack at home.

It seems like restoration had finally came back to the Dakes household. I remember my brother kite had a friend that send goose bumps on me and butterflies in my stomach every time I saw him we both never had many words to say to one another but our body languages and expression towards one another said it all. and I thought wow I am in love truly for the first time you see my relationship with randy was pressure and force and I was more so committed to him and tied to him than in love with him. But this was new I had never been down this path before. So working and preparing to go back to school I had never experience a peace in the family ever before. and this was the first time that I honored my parents and really and truly appreciated them not like in the past were you take them for granted and that they are your parents and they suppose to do the things they do for you but I seen them in a different light and I recognized they hard labor and suffering raising us and I want to do something to show and express my appreciation for them. My first step was to make them proud of me by not cutting corners but sincerely becoming a good daughter I did not want to pull the world over their eyes concerning school grades the whole nine yard. I was standing in the doorway of our new remodel basement around 5pm looking at them and feeling that I wanted to give them the world. I wanted to say it but it was too corny and beside we did not say mushy things to our parents and they did not say them to us either. so I go to I fox downtown and shop for my 11 grade schools clothes AND I am ready I thought about my college and I was going to be a high class secretary. Administration is what I was going to presume. Things are going wonderful and I start feeling sick and could not go a day without these feeling occurring what in the world was happening to me I literally left school every day. one day I came home and my dad came home early he saw me but did not say anything at night I would use the bathroom several times such pressure in my stomach, finally my sisters get wind of this the three eldest from my dad and they decide to take me to the doctor to get pregnancy test. And sure enough I was pregnant. Yes I said how no way I have a period and I have not been active all. of course I forgot that randy the one time randy came to the new house we had relationships but the time before that had been months and time after were months. So all voted that I get an abortion including me. But unfortunately my blood count was so low and I needed a blood transfusion to perform the procedure. Let me correct myself.

I later found out through my mom that my dad suggestion an abortion even though I distance myself from him I was suddenly his little girl again and he was devastated. But my mom being from the south and having her first at 13 I was able to her to handle it just get married that is what they did when she was brought up. It was my pill to swallow and she was going to supply me with the water. Going to the clinic I was not aware that my father new I feared him even though I was Willie baby. the day I went to get the abortion and they turn me around and said they could not do it I made it up in my mind that I was not going back home I cannot hide that fact that I was pregnant from my father any longer. I did not know what to expect from him a whopping a beating a cursing every thought was in my mind. So I left home and went to my eldest mejay house she had 5 children at the time. You see it had become a pattern of the women in my surroundings every sister did not make it pass 16 without getting pregnant under our parents roof but my mom's testimony all her girls had husbands cause papa Willie did not play be believe in shot guns wedding and everyone of us had one all but one up to my pregnancy. so here it t was two to three past and my mom's sends a message that my father said that I had to come home if I was not married or else. now mine you even though I shared with my reading audience that I was working and I had a boyfriend and we were doing or did grown up things that only married consenting people do. There were rules in will house when the streets lights came on everybody had to be in yard or on the porch and be present. We all did our deeds but we did them in secret and behind our father back. My grown siblings never drank liquor in my father present or smoke cigarettes nor use profanity.

Our dad was bad bad Leroy brown baldest man in the whole darn town loll. And still went to church. So back to the story. When my mom call and said my dad said come home I fled from my sister house and went over randy house. oh I forgot did I tell you that when I found out that I was pregnant that I was not seeing randy at the time and that we even stop communicating, but I know that no one had ever been with me but randy. So when my sister found him and call he to tell him he denied it at first because this is October and we had not had contact since early July and before that several months. So him knowing my character he said ok if she says so but I am having my doubts? But long story short. I come to his mother house and she receives me there and we start shacking that what they call it at the time. so my mother comes to randy house and talks with his mom meeting her for the first time, tells her what my father says that if I don t come home he will have me lock up and she and I and all believe him so she pulls out a beautiful wedding ring and encourage her son to marry me. Her adopted father gets involved and here we go in the old red pickup truck 1976 December a week before Christmas to the justice of the peace. In the state I live in 16 you can get married without parent at the time. so it was so busy at city hall the judge that married did not even take us through marriage vows we was brought into his office he was putting on his robe and rushing off somewhere and said two things to us and declare we was married that day. Well we left and I remember that evening I do not know this day but he would not talk and he gave me his bed and he slept on the sofa. That was not our history prior when we were together... but I swallow it I knew I was back in his chains submitting because I had no choice. hey you would say yeah you had a choice your father kept saying come home but what I did not say was my mom had told me that your father do not want you to have it but you need to get married I told her I wanted to stay in school she told me I was a women now. So during the pregnancy I was safe from violence I think I do not remember any major confrontations. So living in my in-law house my sister in law had her man my mother-in-law had who is now her husband of almost 40 years but not at the time so three couples were living in the house at the time but I must say that my mother in law kept an exceptional clean and organize home. Her mange her income very well living offs the government, and she had rules and all abide by them if you wanted to have resident there.

Moving forward it was confirm that you maybe my sons wife and my sister in-law we do not play when it comes to our men so walk lightly. Openly it was stated but my husband was the same he stated that he did not trust his grandfather with me I was a victim and prisoner oh no what was I to do I been sold to randy and threes no getting out of it. So the baby comes in April and we all are excited and happy and it appears that he is in love with me again. So he becomes so controlling that is unbearable. I remembered he was at work he got a job at a gas station and we was so excited I know minimum wage was 2.10 and in some places 2.30 an hour, but I wanted to get out and visit and old school friend and show her the baby I got dress and the baby dress wand we went visiting. I get a call from randy asking me how long had I been gone I knew he was mad and I was in trouble that day. Finally I made it home and he tells me that his mom said I been gone a certain time. He then told me to put the baby down and I was not to take her anywhere and who I think I was I was not allow to make that decision without his permission. So wham the first strike and the blows just continue to come. His mother begs him to stop and release me and this is the beginning of a journey of torment and physical abuse. So 2 months later or more I find an apartment and somehow I convince him to move out of his mother home and he agrees. And we get our first apartment together. I think our rent was 70 or 80 dollars a month no more than that it was a third story high building historical building and we lived on the third floor. His mom was disappointed but there was nothing she could do. We both adjusting to be in full authority away from our parent's roofs. I can say life was bitter and sweet. He became very whorish and argument was constant and I remember him always making up to me and saying he was sorry it became a life-style. I remember constantly regretting this marriage and fighting demons of the mind all I could think about was my brother friend that I had fell in love with and never was able to express it or act it out so I often escape in fantasy world with him over 70%of the time. It kept getting greater the thoughts and I would visit my parents living for the moment that he would stop by because my brother still lives home. Wow I forgot about that that portion in my life concerning Anthony that was or is his name. So here it is my husband is beating now and leaving me so what I do is keep it from the family for various reasons and an in constant begging mode because I do not know how to take care a child and myself. So listen I was very beautiful then but I did not know I always thought otherwise but I was. and going outside of my doors I would be proposition from the time I came out to the time I went in. and sooner or later one particular time during him leaving I needed money and I took a ride with this stranger and he told me that he would help me, be his woman. the bible says that when a man divorce his wife he causes her to committed adultery because according to the bible you are suppose to stay tied together forever. So here it goes my first adultery encounter. I accept the invitation and find myself at this gentlemen home my child and I in his bed and I remember oh how disguising now listen we did not have intercourse but he certainly was rubbing my legs and had stockings on I would not get undress but I did get in his bed it was late I wanted to go home and he told me it was lat and he would take me in the morning but waking up and his private part out I said no you are not the one. So I do cont so after waking up and seeing the position I was in with the stranger, I knew that I did not want to be in that situation and I said that if I make it out of here I will not be back. And so it was God heard my prayers and he took me home as his promise and I did not look back. Moving on my life was headed for a turning point because of this little homeless woman that use to witness to me about becoming a Jehovah Witness' remember listening to her and not understanding why she was old and homeless yet proclaiming her good news. I thought were this poor woman's friends. But anyhow. I shared my experience with the man with no one I mean no one. And things continue to get bad in my marriage and I decided that I would just deal with it. I remember one day I visit a neighbor down the hall from me Ann was her name and she had not long been there but her and I was in the same predicament, meaning outlives and they were the same on every level. I will never forget she talk me into coming down to her apartment just to talk and I remember I was afraid to go but to ashamed to tell her I could not come and I thought I would come and go down to my place before he gets home well. Wrong he came home and I did not here him come into our apartment. and I froze I knew he was coming after me so he said is she here and Ann. said yes and I came out of ANN apartment walking down the hallway and as we were entering into the kitchen he push my head through the glass door and still continue to beat me with a split head. The neighbors got involve and he stops and then took me to the hospital. I remember then you white intern doctor asking question what happen to me he wanted to report him. But as usual I kept silent out of fear and we went home. It was funny whenever he would beat me he would change personalities and become so compassionate towards me wow it is a trip just thinking about it. Living on a 105 and Saint Clair was nothing but violence. There was another time when he left me again and I would get stronger and stronger the more he left was making me feel that I can make it and that I am not afraid to be by myself. well this time he said that he was leaving again and I told him ok but this time give me the key if you are leaving, boy what did I say that for and why did I say that. But to late it was out of my mouth and there was nothing I could do about it. Oh I said it over the phone. So he came home to beat me first then leave for disrespecting him. But this particular time he had his clothes in a carrying bag a paper carrying bag but had a small white and black 22 pistol that he got from his mom I believe and it was sitting on top of the clothes and I quickly grab the gun and had no problem pointing it at him and shooting it. I warn him get back he ignore me I fire the gun. I tell you I fire all the bullets and not one bullet hit him. When he seen the gun was empty he beat me and I do not remember the beating all I know is many officers were standing over me when I came to. Then they proceeded to question me my husband was nowhere to be found I guess neighbors call because of the gun shots. This one cop said all was white men about five or six strap so huge and tall. He said ask me were we married I said yes. he said I do not know what and why this happen but we get many calls and the look of your house it is very clean and in perfect order and your child also, he your husband appear to be a foolish man from the looks of things and when we catch him he will be in big trouble. Then they said mama you cannot stay here tonight do you have a close relative we can take you to and I said yes my sis ill live around the corner sort of speak. but I was not aware that I was blind partially because my face was disfigure and I could not see out of them that is why I was never ask to go to the police station even though I was the one who fired the shots. Oops and I was pregnant also with our second child I do not know how far but pictures was taken in maternity blouse. See this is a book by itself. wow I remember when these things would happen I would recovery in secret cause I did not want my family to get hurt but that time my sister share it with family because of the severity of it. and you think that it could not get any worse but it did later he had left and again and we was hungry and bad off and he came by and it look like he was doing good he had a car and no responsibility and outside arguing with him and this time I think I was seven months pregnant he takes off while I am talking to him and drag me several yards until I fell off and neighbors came and pick me up out of the streets and carry me to my apartment. Is not that something. Well I have my child and my husband rejects the baby because he said his skin was to light and he could not be his. But thank God for moms she told him that his color will change and all babies come out light and chill and he wanted to hear that from his mom.

Yes when my son was born I decided to move from the place we had been living and apply for a house. At that time my faith was high because if it was said I could have it I believe it. So my sister and I went to the realtor with no money no job. actually remembering I visit the realtor while I was carrying my child in the womb and I remember that the man Mr. rice was so atoned by me coming into his office to discuss buying a home that that he was tickle and he share with me all that I had to do to go about being a home owner. So when the time was right I saved up 500 and put it in my saving and I was told just leave it there the banks just need to see that I have a savings. So yeah folks in 1979 I became a home owner. I tell you God did it. The house was perfect beautiful just move in everything was in tic and very modern. Again no job, my husband had a job but his money did not go toward it because he did not believe it could be done. at the time of the purchase of the new home I was 18 turning 19 and somehow or another my name was not on the deed, my husband name was cause he had a job and he was 21 years old and I thought oh I do not matter we will be together what does it matter. So we move in the house I was the first of my father's children to become a home owner wow! But things change and I wanted to go back to school and get a job I had ideas lots of them and vision but my husband could not see it or agree to me working he was very insecure he did not want me to do neither one. So it was a fight every time I would try to do work or school. I was in bondage so in order to feel like I had a life I got very involve in the Jehovah witnessing bible home study groups and he did too much reject to it but I had better not push it to far on him in other words when it became a bother to him no question about it he would shut it down. so this religious encounter kept me content from trying to do anything with my life because there were a whole lot of women that did what I did and that was nothing and it was alright and acceptable. But oops in my contentment I became pregnant and my husband was not thrill about it neither was I or at least I do not remember having those feelings. Well he said to me to get rid of it and first I did not think that he was serious but he was so I found a doctor that would do the procedure. and I remember that he had to hospitalize me because of the anaemia blood condition that I had at the time's remember being admitted on a Sunday and that I had second thoughts about it and I wanted to come home and when calling my husband he was very mad and curse at me for asking him to come and get me so I went to sleep and when I woke up they had took my child. I felt horrible wow. I remember my husband being ashamed because we were having a third child and he said he did not want me pregnant every year. And I told my mom because I had took on his feeling and she spoke never be ashamed you are married you are to never be ashamed you are married. Well little did my husband and I know that that decision that we made to terminate our child was a price that we did not see coming. I stuck with the Jehovah witness and my husband grew farther away from me. There was no love between us he showed every day that he resented being my husband. listen I was warned by the Jehovah witness lady not to abort my child but I did not heed and hell came to our house the beating got greater the cheating the sexual diseases he would bring. I saw him as the devil. But I was ignorant internally I escape through imaginations of being married to my brother friend whom I fell in love with the summer of 1976, that was my escape. So I was sinning as well because I was lusting after another in my heart while married. But anyways the separation finally came. one day received a call from my husband and he told me that he had to do him first or help his self first before he could help us his family I disagreed I said that we was to walk the journey together he said no I am leaving you today. I did not believe that it was over between us. But it was.

Yes it was over that man came home and pack his bags and left. I was not frantic about it because this was his behavioural all the time so. Wow I could get a job now without no hack so that is what I did got me a hotel and I was so very concern about not losing our home and so I was looking for all kind of resources to help from one hotel job to another and by the way for a moment my Jehovah witness practicing went out the window for a while I was in the panic zone. So here I land a Job in the downtown area and mean while I am getting use to being single he Y my family was Baptist you can believe and sin ant the same time. They model was he left you so you have a right to get you someone else his rights are all gone. And look this is what every sister of mine done so it was the norm at that time for me. The threat started coming from the husband you cannot bring a man to my house. So he no longer threatened me he acted out.

One Sunday afternoon I was off from work 6 0r 8 months into the legal separation that was issue on his part to me I decided to have my first date. I knew my husband was dating and my ignorant self call my husband and ask him could I have a date I been asked out he responded by saying do not call me I could not careless. So I took that as a yes even been married I knew nothing about men. Well the date has begun I had a house full of people because my sister was staying and her children at the time with me to help pay bills but she was gone at the time so just me and children. So my guest comes over and sit to watch the game and shortly after the visit we get a knock on the door and my husband is at the door he pulls out a gun and put it in the man's face to intimidate him and then snatch me out the door and drives me around the corner and pulls the trigger to shoot me and the cops yell to him put your gun done and get out of the car. Wow saved in a nick of time. They take him off and I go back home and my date is still there which later becomes my last child father. Well we continue to date and I find out that I am pregnant and now my boyfriend whom I am pregnant by moves me out or I should say I move out and he becomes just as abusive if not more than my husband and I am being toss back and forth with emotions from the two of them threatening from one day to day basis. Wow could this be really happen no support system I had because my family was crazy and I did not wasn't them to get hurt or catch a case. So I kept it to myself all the miseries that I was encountering. Now the house my husband name was on it even though he did not put a dime toward it sold the house to his girlfriend sister. yes he would not let me stay in it saying he would kill and trying to do just that my mom call me one day and said give the house to him you can get another one. So when she said that I release it. also I remember he said that my husband he made a mistake and that he wanted his family back and that things will be different if he came back and I told my mom and she said no. no you cannot go back to him seeing that he knows that you have had another man and when he gets angry with you that will come up. His history with violence brought him a strike from my mother. See she was not just being meant to him she was concern about my safety. So again I took her advice and till this day I am not sure that that was the right advice for me because he change so dramatically and he is not that same person today he was yesterday. Now getting back to the new man in my life and my new child I was so disappointed that I let things play out itself I do not have to tell the details but it was the same story over again and notice these men kept me from my folks neither one was family friendly. So now with three children opps I get pregnant again by my baby daddy and this time I find the same doctor and tell him that he has to perform an abortion for me. The doctor tell me on one condition you have to declare to the state of Ohio that you are mentally ill that is the only way the state will allow me because you are under the age limit I might of been 22 or 23 but anyhow. It was done and I felt good about it you see when you do evil or bad it gets easier and easier each time you act it out.

So five years into the relationship without no intervene from my ex it was like he drop off the face of the earth concerning me. You see he and my baby father had had many run in s and I did not know about most of them but the one that I did not know about that came out much later down the road was that once they were at this bar and when Donn Lee told my then husband Randy Perry that randy son and mines was his child and that we were together while we was married and together can you imagine a thing I never knew the man existed but Donn Lee wanted to get back at randy for pulling the gun out on him at my house. How cruel that was of donn to tell randy that lie and as a result of that randy stop trying to have a relationship with the children he had with me. And when he did reach out which was very seldom he would never ask for his san lil randy, all because donn told him that my son was his. And remember in the beginning of the story when I told you big Randy has an issue with our son when he was born because he was light in complexion. Well donn was a very light man and randy was very dark. But I will note that I never knew any man other than my husband during our marriage when we were together. So this lie causes my son to never know his father at all. Silly my husband Randy felt when his son became the spitten image of his dad in appearance. Randy later apologize to lil Randy when he turn 18 years old they told that he cried and was very sorry for not being in and apart of his life. Well back to Donn he terrorise me for many years even when he moved away but what got me out of that entanglement is when one day I went to his apartment to pick up our son Lee and I quest his was not expecting me to arrive so soon and when I did there was this woman very pregnant there and I had seen her before and knew her and Donn would be at the same bar together. And there it was he was expecting a child with her here he was controlling my life and home from a distance and all the time was living a double life and that was my way out with boldness and courage for myself to stand up against this giant that was bullying me in my life. So I told him that no need to explain I get it and see you. I tell you I was hollering on the inside because I finally had my freedom papers and I was taking them and walking out of prison with them. And at that point I gave him no more power over me. So I really began to my thing because for me I was an adult for the first time in my life that I made all the decision concerning me and my house. So now here comes the mistakes and many that is to be made by me. There was relationships one after another none of which I am or was proud of. Still not finding an atmosphere or home like experience in the term of family yet. Well my children are 12, 11 and 8 and my daughter is going through a lot of changes or I should say giving me the most challenges in my life at the moment and it is truly taking me over the top. To the point where the life that I left from the abusive relationships was starting not to look so bad and I wish I was back in them. I did not know that the bad choices that I made with allowing men to come to my house would have a great and negative impact on my children especially my daughter. Well without getting into her life I will just say my grandchild was born to me at the age of 31. I was seeking love and she was seeking to be love and while all this is happening. I was first up I had money in the bank car a 1 credit and buying the kids what they needed and wanted. But let me back up for a minute. We going back to 1984 yeah I cannot leave out that year. Yeah I am 24 and I was in school fulltime managing a food chain store no complaints money and career wise but my daughter going through what I thought beginning stages of puberty. But while I am rocking this freedom life and doing me.

I decided to involve myself in man in prison that I knew from being a friend of my older brother and this guy was actually good for me. He was positive the whole 3 year relationship I think we had. I had the comfort without the drama so I went back to my Jehovah witness teaching the whole nine yards I thought and felt that I was on top and when this man comes out of jail he would help me with my children so I thought I told yall that I did to know much about men. Cause I made so many bad choices and none that value me and love me I loved all abut did not get the level of love I so again three years went by I am on top of the world job school boyfriend MK and wham my father's dies the beginning of and then my aunts die April of the year now I am dealing with these tragedy but my concerns is my mother and my man in jail. I handle the death of my father well I surprise myself but I was holding on to my faith that was taught but all the time saying just don't let my mom die so my mom was a lady that what I call a positive spirit my only memories of her was uplifting encouraging and always positive and happy. So here it is my man is coming home the same day that we get the burial date for my mother. Yes she died seven months after my dead the week that my friend is release from prison what I cannot tell you the emotions I had during that time. I remember plainly

I hope he understands that I cannot do intimacy at all my mom just died. But I did not have to worry about that because he never call me or showed up and all I could say was wow. Of course I lied to myself and said oh he is just giving me some time she know I love her. But no that was not true he did not call or show up period. And I thought I was consistent and faithful and loyal to him for three years what. And I blank out. The Lord protected from grieving and sorrow concerning my mom because 1987 had been a rough year as far as my heart. So I pain more for the failed relationship think than for my mom. We talked every single day was the best of friends and it was well with my soul because she was out of the suffering. You see she battle with diabetes and her leg was cut off. Her story was some like mines but she handle her rejection better than I did she had great wisdom. So we all thought that she would pass before my father because she had so many bought with death but he went first and she decided to follow I believe to this day by choice. So after reality of the entire year had set in I started to dated again and no one was interested in a commitment just a good time and the last choice was a man by the name of Tim that sent me running. By this time I went downhill lost everything had very low self esteem. I let my brother talk me into leaving my position at my job and start a restraint for him at the same time another relative had me work for him so like what was guaranteed to work for hustlers and they were too out there for me I could not hang I did not belong at all. So I pick from rite aid store I was a clerk there and he came in on a regular basis well I brought him to my house and I thought finally a man that cares and is committed little did I know that he was as close to a serial killer there was. So I bring him in and we move from the present place to a new place to start a beginning and four months in the new place this guys begins to beat me to know end it was unbelievable he picks me up from work nothing out of the ordinary our drive home and he turns in to a monster I do not know what happen no argue at all and he had to be high off some crazy stuff because began to beat me in public like a monster no one person help or call the police. We were eye vision of a police station he did not care and I know he was going to kill me that night but God said it was not my time so a police car drove by and I jump in front of it and when the police car stop and the officer got out they look like giants and this guy did not care he was still trying to get me. They took me home and him to jail and the next day or when I went to court to prosecute him the female judge did not like the fact that when he spoke and lie I said to her that is not true she dismiss the case. I still had a prosecutor appointment ant the prosecutor said to me do you know who you are messing with. I cannot reveal his file to you or I will get in trouble but I will tell you one thing he thought a toddler a baby out of a three story building on purpose. The he said I hope that is enough for you to run and leave this guy along and I said it was but he did not leave me along. Thing guy was big strong and serve prison time I found out that he slice his mother husband 48 times and beat him and left him for dead I can tell you I was purple black and blue. This guy Tim took the cake from all the others he began to show up at my school I was going to beauty school at the time come in and grab me out of there he would-be hiding in the bushes at night waiting for me and jump on the hood of my car. This man would kick the door in and state that when he finds us that he will kill us. You talk about freight we were hiding in the attic of the house minutes before I got wind of him coming I bust out all the light bulbs in the house my daughter had a new born child we ran in attic in hiding God hide all of us my two sons daughter andl that night he came to kill the police would just miss him they told me that I could kill him and if they see him that they will kill him. I had a gun I met a trucker guy that told me how to saw off a shot gun bullet and cut with a knife to fit it into a 22 pistol so I did just what he said my brother offer me a 38 pistol but I was afraid of0it power so I took his wife 22. But one evening doing overtime I pulled in my driveway and I could not get out of the car for some reason that was the Holy Spirit giving me insight. So I stayed in the car and stayed and there he was he came out of the bushes yelling now it is about 3'oclock in the morning. I put the car in reverse and he hops on top of the hood of the car. He lays horizontal so I would stop driving because I could not see where I was going. But that did not stop me I know it was my life at stakes so I drove finally he felt off and I ran his entire body over and drove to the police station and told them what had happen and I said to them I do not know if he is alive or dead. They did not hold me they told me to go home. And from that time I never heard anything from him. One Sunday morning I was driving not to long after that incident and he was standing at the bus stop with a cane he was cripple. But truthfully I was still haunted by his actions and was not comfortable. So I said that I was moving out of state I waited until I passed the state board for beauty license pass 98 percent got test score in April and on June 3rd 1991 i was headed to Detroit Michigan. Yeah I turn the key to my new place never being in it before I was so desperate for a new beginning that I did not care that it was Detroit. Well what a turning point in my life so off to Detroit I went my three children my dog and I my brother Mike drove us in a U-Haul to meet our new destiny. So now I am a license beautician and I am on my way to a life that I could not even imagine. Oh by the way I forgot to men-tioned that when my mom die I walk away from following the Jehovah witness group. Because the following week after her burial I had a bible study in my home and my group leader that was over the studies told me these word ah Liz you know that your mama is not in heaven or going to heaven. And I was stunned for the first time I did not like what I was hearing. I was baffle at her words and I told her to leave and I no longer wanted a study. No all these years I study as a witness 11 to be exact I was comfortable believing that and telling others that but this was my mom big mama Mrs. pan, this was her God and belief no that was not sitting well with my heart. So readers I forgot to warn you that I was back tracking for a moment down memory lane. So that was in the fall of 1987 when my mom pass.

So any way across the street from my house they were build-ing a brand new church very large and modern it was call Zion hill Baptist church. And now they had a lot of community thing to offer the children in the neighbourhood and my two sons to go since other children from the hood would be there. So they ask me if they could go to church and I said no because even though I stop study-ing I was not into the church because they taught us that they were Satan worshippers and there place of worship was really defile and demonic. so anyways my sons insisted and did not want to tell them no so I said ok but I am going with you and I will sit in the back and they went to the front of the church and toward the end of the ser-vice they people was praising the name of Jesus in continuance and I said in my heart who are you Jesus I do not know you. Because in our practice we only said Jehovah and skip the name of Jesus. So I heard a response from my heart I am Jesus, then I said I am alone and I have no one and he responded am here and I always been with you and I will not leave you have Me. I felt good after that and did not believe any of the teaching that I was taught from that point on from the Jehovah witness hall and the people. But at the end of the service my two sons wanted to join the church and I did not know that it was my son that wanted to join the church because I was seated in the back. But the Pastor call for the parent of the children so I can up and allow them to join the church and received the pray. So they joined the church did not know that my children was used by God to later on bring me into a relationship with Jesus. So we moved in the city not knowing I would be moving to one of the most thriving drug neighbourhood. So I got the kids settle and I went to work at my sister salon as her assistant and shampoo girl. Her salon at the times was thriving one of the hottest shops in the city. I was working night and day and I got freighted for leaving my children at home by themselves so often. You know a mothers insight I knew that something just did not sit right me being gone so long. Drug addicts prostitutes in the house right next to mines so amazing but home owners and families on the street as well working people. I thought I did not move up here to throw my sons into these people command and demand Lord please help me! So I may a vow to the Lord if you keep my children safe I will serve you. I remember panicking every day on the news tragedy I said I just cannot swallow death I do not want it near me or near anyone I am connected to. So I know that people preach against coming to the Lord because of fear but that is exactly what made me come to him. So I forgot to share that the week we move in our house my boys were so not feeling Detroit and I did not know what to do to get them to accept the transition. So I went back to Ohio and convince there old friends to come and spend two weeks with us so they parents let their friends come I agree to bring and take them back home and a funny experience happen on our way while riding the greyhound bus I met a priest that was on the bus and we had conversation as to why I was moving to Michigan and he listen but then he put his hands on my forehead and begin to pray in a foreign language so I thought but what I know it to be know was speaking in tongues. Yes a Caucasian male in long black priest attire like of the catholic but not sure his religion. But anyway he prayed over me for a good while and the audience on the bus began to laugh and mock what was happening to me, my first reaction was I was honour but I quickly became ashamed of the saying that was being said. So I never gave that much thought I really forgot about it but remember it later what I really meant to me and why did he do that to me. So the boys come and stay and children get comfortable and the same habits I did or had in Ohio I brought them to Detroit, the habit I am talking about is having poor judgement of character and my daughter and I both look like was in the same bubble of disappointments and rejections and failures. So wow the shop in jumping I learning skills and tades developing a love for the profession getting addictive to the atmosphere meeting people and escaping from home on the other hand my children are being and becoming a product of the environment because the people became the new daddy and mama. So one day I never forget that I would get so frustrated not having a parking space every night when I came home because of the drug traffic next door so I took beer bottles as many as I could find and broke them in front of my house to reserve me a spot when I came in at night. I also went to the detectives just around the corner from house and ask them to do something about the activity next door to me. No response so we wrote a letter to the white house and told them what was happening and after that we had no problem they clean up the street drove the people away fix up the house and a school teacher move next door to me. That street became a quiet street I stay there 9 years and home was never broke into neither of our neighbours homes was children play from sun up to sun down never no shooting or crimes it was if God his fence us in and kept us safe and a great community. But while working in the shop I met a lot of Christians and they would invite me to their churches and I would go but I was sinning on a daily basis but now here is the scene you remember I told you when we moved to Detroit we brought a dog with us. Well we brought our family dog king and my landlord did not know that we would be bringing a dog with us and told us that we would have to get rid of our dog. So this was a real concern of mines and I share it with the ladies at the salon because I was going to move from the house if we could not have the dog. so the nail tech said hey my boy friend father have a space for your dog until you find a new place to move because folks I tell you I was moving, so I sent the dog over to Buford's house not knowing that his would be my next boyfriend. Weeks goes by and it is time to take the kids to visit the dog. Oh it was such a long journey we live on the west side and he lived on the eastside. This was in the early summer and little did I know that the nail tech was playing match maker at the same time helping out our pet dilemma. so we get over there and there is a party going on and the yard and house was full of people and we was introduce and met the quest that was there and we did not stay long and we left. Later Buford call me and we talk and I liked that he was single and working and had his own home that was very nice but that was all initially. I thought he was too old for me he was 12 years older than me but that was not the main issue his hair was all gray and he was so mature with very string features so serious and big in statute just I never dated his type on no basis. but the conversations were constant and he came to see me and ask me to move in with him my kids and all the dog and the grandbaby and I said with no hesitation or thought no. not knowing that I hurt his feeling and his self-esteem because I did not know then that that was out of his character and he meant it sincerely and I had no regards and I literally crushed him. so we had dinner and he and his friends left and little did I know that that was going be the end of his presueing so days went by an I had the opportunity to chew on all that Buford had said to me in days and I became attracted to the silence he was giving me. And then that's when I discover that I wanted him to pressure me so I had to humble myself and make the first move by calling him. He took my calls but the fire he had towards me was not there but he was curious to see if we had a destiny together. Wow I can say that I had a great relationship with him let none that I had in the past. This is what I was talking about a committed relationship. We plan to marry twice and each time the death of my sister delay and postpone it and other matters which occurred. but I had came to the conclusion that I was in love for the first time and all the others relationships that I had was not love like I thought. This relationship gave me security safety and provision something that I never had in any of the relationship I was always the one who was giving in the relationship on every level of an relationship. But one major issue stood as a block or a sore thumb in our relationship was he was an alcoholic this was my first. sadly to say even though I pick some loser none drank on a daily basis or kept liquor in the home when it happen it was very few an only occasional. so this was all new to me so I slow down with the marriage planning and I started going to my sister Louise church which was around the corner from the salon and Buford and I would go together and each time I would bring a new rule or commandment to the relationships because of the convictions I would be feeling one day over to his house I told him we would not be engaging into married people activities and I thought he would say ok that it this relationship is over. But he said instead that ok I respect you I will not bother you this will not push me away in other words. So I thought that wow he is willing to date me still with this demand he must be the one for me. I remember hoping Lord deliver clean him of that drinking demon so he and I can keep married but no that is not how things turn out. Maybe two more times he came to church with me and drifting came between us. While Jesus was working on me and I desire more and more of him until I had Jesus in me all around me. Weeks had gone by and I call him or he call me and I could tell had been drinking but he wanted to see me and I wanted to see him. So I went to his house after church and the screen door was open and I walk in and I told him that I was there and he and a lady came down the stairs and he introduce the two of us and she ask me what was I to him and I said his girl friend and she said so was her. and her presence brought about authority ownership and ruler ship and he told me and her that he loved the both of us. I told him to tell her to leave and she told him to tell me to leave and guess what he obey her and told me to leave you talking about hurt we dated three years I had keys to his house the kids and I spent the summer at his house and the winter at mines. What is going on I thought oh I will forgive him he is just drunk I left the first thing the next day I was back and he told me that Liz this lady and I go back a long ways we bought this house together see that dog in the back yard that our dog so on and so forth I kick holler and scream how could this be we only been away from each other 2 or 3 weeks. He said that they been together 12 years oppose to our 3. I remember driving over there that morning and the Spirit of the Lord spoke it to my heart that it was over and that he was closing that door. I did not accept it my heart sank inside of me and I was lifeless. day in and day out I had a broken heart nothing could sooth it reading my word or going to church encouraging words there was no medicine on earth that could help me I could understand I tried to reject the pain I was in agreement with the final decision all I wanted to was to be healed and to go on with my life but when you give something that you do not have a right to give away like your heart. I am not talking about my love or my feelings this was something new. He won my heart and I gave it to him. I was ill sick anything that hit the human body and contaminate it was happening to me. Real deal death was on me trying to take me I did not want to go I told the Lord to let me live I got these kids let me live Lord. So many discussions I had with God. God show me I gave up my rights for my life. Because according to the bible I was a pearl and the bible says do not cast your pearls among swine because they will not know the value of it and they will trample on them and smashed the pearls.

And that is what happen to me. I remember pressing my way to work after crawling up the wall the night before fighting to live. I went to work and I had two very old ladies hair to do that day they were sister and I do not think ever been married. I tried to get out of doing their hair I thought that they was strange and a little scary to me one was very dark complexion and she look masculine to me they both wore head scarves and had mustaches. But they conduct was very feminine and more like old great grandmas. So she said baby what wrong I was shame to tell them because I knew that they was in the church and beside it did not think that they could relate to my situation. but I went on and told them and the one most masculine oh honey I know exactly what you are experiencing I went through the exact, do you mind if my sister and I pray for you I said sure I would not tell anyone no I was desperate. So they prayed for me those two sisters prayed for me and what I was tormented with for 2 months by the next day it was gone. I thought God I would have never thought that my blessing and deliverance would come through these two old ladies. Beware of blessing in disguise you do not know who is holding your blessing. My kids had they mama back what had happen between Bufford and I had affected my kids. They was very hurt buy it. So the sky was blue again in my life and not gray. Of course I was going to be a good girl. I started going to church every time the door open and reading my bible every time at 10 at night stop watching TV cut all the hanging buddies a loose. I started by gospel music I have move from shampoo girl to getting my own booth and I started praying for folks and taking folks to church have church in the salon just gone extreme for this new found life. And I should have know but I was a babe in Christ in did not have on my whole amour I was reckless and wild in the Lord. But God allow that beginning for me because I would not change any of it for nothing. The devil said I going to put a hindrance in her path. See I did not know about retaliation. well one Monday morning as you know hairdressers are off and my sister ask me to go to home depot I think at the time she is a professional decorator along with being a stylist and salon owner at the time and I said yeas. Well we went and spent the whole day on my way home driving down livernois the street stopping at every light it is rush hour I am hungry trying to get home and fix dinner for the children and I notice this guy keeps looking at me and he is laughing and I am laughing because I was devouring the popcorn because I was so hungry. And we kept getting stuck at the same lights so he asks me to pull over. I know yall is saying not again when is she going to learn but be patience I pull the car over and I was not interested I told him that my life what pretty boring and I cut out everything and I am a true follower of Christ and he said that is fine here is my number. So I took it and he said that he was in the medical profession and gives him a call if I needed medicine he could get me discount from where he work I said fine I did not feel pressure I was smiling because I felt pretty that day, so I tuck the number away and forgot about it. Down the road one day I woke up with the worst head pain you could imagine I had sinus problems really bad. And I call a friend over to take me to the doctor and instantly I thought about the number I got from bobby gee he answer and told me to send my friend by he had the perfect medicine for me.

So my friend went and while he was gone my best friend call and I told her what I was experiencing and she prayed for me and I was instantly healed and when my friend got back I did not need the medicine. So later I call him to thank him for the medicine and that was all and I think he call me back it is not clear because it was 20 years ago or more. but we talk a few times and again we had a date to meet on Monday to watch Monday night football my children now was 16 15 12 somewhere around there and I wanted them to be involved if he is voted in or out I value there opinion at this point bobby gee walks in the door and the children gather in the kitchen and says no right off the bat. They said that he was to cool a ladies' man and no see he watch for a little and he left. And I told my sister about the visit and he came by the shop and I cannot remember her respond but it was not positive but not negative pretty much a pause on her evaluation. And I told him the children give not give him a thumbs up. But anyway the onversations between him and I for 2 months and basically therelationship was mostly spent on the phone I met his family in one visit and after meeting his family he got on his knees and ask me to marry him. He pulled out his mother wedding ring she had from his father and she.

His father was deceased at the age of 12 and since he had a new stepfather. So the rings were put away until bobby gee found me. Well I was truly surprise at the proposal and he in addition read a little note to me how the ring was to go on the finger of a saved woman and he thought I was as saved as they came because nothing was going in my life but God work and family that was all. No outside activities or adventures were I intrigue with at that time. so that night on our way back to my house he told me that he was not perfect but his imperfections he would keep them from me and respect me in my faith and keep ungodly things away from our home and relationship. And I thought oh he is honest and that is attracting me right now his honesty. So I put it out there to friends and family and some was excited an d some flat out said no absolutely not. A sister said she thought he had a femine side, the children said he had a criminal side. My best friend at the time said wed was un evenly yoke in other words he was the devil and I was the saint. And I took all of it in. and I thought well I want a husband I will be soon 34 and if not now then when. My mama told me not to go back to my first husband when he wanted me back because he would not be able to forgive me and I listen but I hear that is a great guy now very responsible and respectable, so in the back of my mind did I give-up to soon ah not sure but this opportunity that is in my face I want to take deep thought concerning it so I will not lose out. so you know people I said yes I will marry you so he was willing to wait until our wedding night and that was a big plus for him his family was not sure because they said my children was older kids and that could become an issue later on so he and I went to the justice of the peace and they would not marry us because a technicality on the spelling of my name not have the same spelling and so disappointed he and I were we came home and made believe that the wedding took place. I should have recognize the sign that maybe we should not be getting marry but no I did not and would not listen. We had plans to correct the spelling error and go back as soon as possible. So the kids went away for the weekend and when they were to return there would be a new step dad in the house. He wanted me and my kids wanted so I felt pulled on trying so hard to make the peace in the house. just a few days that went by I went to buy groceries and I bought a large amount of them and I notice that I was in my bedroom closet and discover pops bottle pop or soda on the floor of my closet and who knows what else and I did not know how they got there and I ask him, bobby hey do you know that there is pop in the closet he said yes I put it there so they will not drink it from us. I know this may seem small to some of your readers but this was huge to me I had never done such a thing before when we ran out of food we just replaced them that is how it always worked in my house. So I return the pop and told him I will get more if we run out. So two weeks almost to the date we go to get marry again a friend of mines refer this pastor in the city to marry us and he did bobby was fine with the way things were but I told him you have to leave if a legal wedding does not occur so we went to a church this time and was married the next he and I was going to file ours taxes because it was tax time and as we were about to go he had no shirt on a leather jacket and that he was sweating his eyes were big and I am thinking what the heck is going on? Wait who are you? then no work not going to work know when he and moved in together he had two jobs working at hospital wearing labs coats I mean I was proud to be on this fellow arms, ok. What no explanation I quit they not fair their not giving me enough hours. So not even a month this man is jobless I am going to work and he is still in my bed not a good sign at all. Then next his car is broke now you taking me to work. Oh well by now I know what is happening. But I am save now I got to think the bible way what and how Jesus says to do it. So now prayer is going get this fellow on track so I think but remember yall I was still new in my Christian walk they consider you a babe if you are less than three years in the faith so I made a huge I made a huge mistake I thought. I can tell you out of all the relationships this is the one that made me the best because I grew so much spiritually and naturally. well I was only a year and 4 months older than he was but he made me feel like I was ten years older than him because of the lack of priorities he was very irresponsible he never ask for a bill or ask what do we need to pay or quite frankly gave me money for the bills even when he worked whatever that was given I gave it back to him after all his money was gone. So I got to a point that if his money supplied his needs I was good with that because my money was just enough to make do. so here now my two sons is living with me while my daughter has moved out and no longer with one child but two children a girl and boy. so to keep from breaking from running to household I really clinch tight to my church and my get away was work and church I remember wishing that Bobby Gee would disappear I did not want a divorce but I wanted him off of the planet earth I thought if he had a accident that would be my way out and I thought these thoughts daily. the women calling the house he not coming home till morning and my sons did not like it I remember that my son heard a conversation bobby and I had over the phone and he was ease dropping on the line and he spoke up and told him that he would hurt him and he meant it if he disrespect me in any way. And by this time my son was very huge at the time and without fear.

So I had to keep are arguments very discreet. But bobby kept on living reckless he told me if I would go to the bars and participate in the doing that he done he would not do the things he do. He also told me to my face yea when I am mad at you I cheat on you that is how I get back at you. I said wow he really do not know me because I came from such abuse in my past I became as hard as a rock and can take or leave that what my attitude but he only know the church girl he did not know that I had a past and side that could pluck his hearts strings. But I had to compress that side of me and me let him release enough rope that he would eventually hang himself. And I will get to that part in a little while. I forgot to mentioned back in 1993 when I was single my sister and I went to a revival that had been on the radio and signs and wonders was happening in the meetings of the revival and this one night that we went the place was pack and I was praying and walking the floor and the prophetess that was overseeing the service was tell the people to pray in their holy language which I could not do and I remember talking to God and Jesus and saying that Lord I do not know how to this thing this woman is requesting and I cannot fake it but I want to be obedient and I was so overwhelmed because I heard so many people speak in this language and I tried to make sounds and mimic the sounds bi to Jesus that this is not right I cannot fake this thing so I heard the lady say just a few more seconds and we will have our break through and I literally said out of my mouth goo goo ga ga and I repeated it again and in frustration I said Lord I cannot do this and then the next thing I know is that I was standing and I open my eyes and seen everyone in the room sitting and you could hear a pin drop and I only I was standing and a sound was coming out of my mouth and I had no controlled of it and it was if someone was turning the sound down lowering it until there is no sound left to be heard and when the sound from heaven ended I heard the prophetess from the pulpit say there it is that is our answer. And I could not tell what happen to me was I in my body or out of it. And that experience never happens to me again. I tried to have it happen to again but it was clearly a divine interruption on God's behalf concerning me and his will for my life. audience can't you see the trails that Jesus is leading me on the man on the greyhound bus prays for me in public in tongues, my two sons joining church and the Lord speaks to my heart and tell me that he is with me and has always been there and then back in the sixties my dad having prayer meeting at our house and choir rehearsal with all types of musical instruments. Now it all beginning to make sense all these challenges are for my prepping. so now back to bobby one hot day in the summer I am at work and I get a call from my kids telling me that a lady call the house and she said that she is pregnant with bobby child and is due any day now and tell your mama this and that her name was Annette and that she work on the job with him. So while they are telling me I must have swallowed a brick I was trying to stay calm I was working on my client so I had to keep my composure so quietly I so I call him and tell him what the kids just said so I gets off work and discover that every bit of it is true. So the lady Annette and I are talking and her whole motive was to separate us and he said he did not want to be with her and told her that that was to bad yeas I know he was something else had more mercy and compassion for his mistress than he did. but if she had not tried to hurt me further than what I was he would have been her property that night but I told her when I get ready to release him to you I will.

l but right now he stays mine cause you ain't taking nothing from me, you see they both work at this hospital on nights they both was married and however it started they begin to become a couple at work I now know that during Christmas time he had me buy her a Christmas present. They pulled names iDon the job and he pulled her name. bobby live two lives this woman told me that he lived with her and her sons call him daddy and he take them to soccer games etc, I told her how could this be I see him off to work and I am home when he comes in from she said I do not now but he lives here so I was just listening to her then she said he told me that he does not like black women and that was going to leave you eventually. And I said well his mother is black and sisters is black and I forgot to mention that he has a daughter before the two of us got together and married. So when she said that because she was a white woman. I decided to keep him out of spite. She threat him that she would give the baby away from adoption and he told her to do he did not care and we did not hear from her until 7 years later when her husband past away and she wanted her child to know her real father which was bobby. During the time she was with my husband I guess her husband and her were separated. So maybe internally bobby was stress and we you thought things could not get worse but they did. Of course he left that job and found a job closer well things settle down just a bit and when I say just a bit I mean whatever that man was doing it just was not uncover yet. At this particular time my granddaughter was about 7 or 8 I am not sure but bobby would help in getting her to and from the day care because everyone in our household and including my daughters house was working yeah! So of course I would be dropped off daily and pick up by bobby. One day I received a call from my daughter and she share with me that she was Bobby and a lady in my car and she tried to be nice as possible as she could by telling me. But for her to call me she had seen them together several times and could not take it seeing her mom being taken advantage of, because she knew that I was carrying the entire load. So when I confronted him he said that she was his friend's wife and they were paying him to pick her up and besides he was always in the car with them. But he was being a gentleman by allowing her to sit in the front seat. So I said ok and I of course drop it. But did not forget it. So the year of 2000 was ending and both sons moved out at almost the same time. My youngest son lee left for college and little Randy move in with his soon to be wife and my daughter got married all in the fall of 2000 to a man that seem to be stable enough to handle her and now three kids. But any ways bobby would always tell me when your kids leave our marriage will start oh he was very selfish. So we decided to down size and move into smaller place but still big enough for our family. So little did I know that I would be moving just around the corner from Bobb's long time lover. But we moved and it do not seem that it was a difference that that it was the two of us no change as I could see it, so now it is time for bobby family to come and live since mines were gone. And remember I share that he had a daughter prior to our marriage well now she is 16 and popping her mama can't do anything with her and was ready to send the child to us. I ain't going to lie I did not want her to come at all. One day when she visit us at the age of 8 or my first time meeting her she cried and told bobby that she wanted to stay with us and that she did not want to go home to her mother. I thought because my sons and their friends were over that day and I had at that time my decease sister child with me. She stays the course of 3 years with me but they were the same age and she thought wow I want to live here you see she was the only child she had no sibling her mother had a blood disease and was bed and hospitalize most of the time and her mom boyfriend was her main caregiver at the time. but I did not give bobby a ok for his child to stay I had no words but dealing with her mom was such a trip I thought no way I want this but when it was time for the child to leave the child doll fell out of the car and when I pick the doll up it was a real voodoo doll with pins and needles stuck on every area of the doll. Then I open the child book bag to put the doll inside and the child had several books on witchcraft and I thought wow this is very strange. And I never forgot that exposure but sadly I never made a connection why I stayed sick all the time very bad head pains breathing issues and doctor could not detect it so much that two sisters died and I did not go to any of their funeral  because I was sick crawling the floors most of the time and my oldest son would hold me like an infant while bobby would be out and doing whatever. I remember him saying with n o compassion that I don't want no sick woman not wife he said woman and I am not with this stuff man. Once I was having breathing issue and crawling the floor and I was reaching for him to help me and he push me and starred at me. Now that I will never forget. Now back to the new move between us in our upstairs flat. I was so sick they was burying my sister my brother call which is a minister and said just rest do not worry about coming to the funeral this was my mom first child he prayed for me and I rested and look at the television. This man told a story how there was a man that was suffering from severe head pains and he got prayer and discover that he had poison in his blood from a bad tooth and I thought Lord could this be my circumstances so that night pain could really bad and my children gather around me was watch me suffer and I told them that I was going to find a doctor in the morning that will or would pull my tooth but as I pray that night I thank God for revealing that to me through the TV and I prayed Lord whatever power or spirit that is sending this affliction to me I send it back to the sender in the name of Jesus Christ our Lord.

I said those words and sure enough we found a doctor that would pull the teeth when so many said no and I tell you that the blood that came out from those teeth all that poison that was in the blood cause my head to hurt left. I stayed on the antibiotics and I know that the Lord sent that answer to me. Well moving on back to bobby and his daughter Makkey. He flat out told me that she is coming to stay with us so get use to it. The day she move in I was at work that day and when I'd got home she brought garbage to my house the things were really bad and I thought no she brought a cat. I said what a cat I do not do cats. And she was in Gotha everything that she own was black her nails clothes. her movies everything she stood talk as her dad and she was solid as any man. we or he gave her the room down the hall and you could her screams coming from the room horror screams and he told her that she have to keep that down. She told him that she wanted her fiends to come and he said that she could have friends and I told him absolutely not I have to get to know her before I could or would allow her friends to come. That was a big match but I won that one. I never it was the fourth of July and I felt like a prisoner in my house and I notice that he did not spend time with her neither and I did not want to leave my house because I did not want her to take over so I was there as much as possible so I told bobby that she was a witch and he did not take me serious but he reply all it is just a phase she is going through and she will grow out of it. And I thought that is how you going to look at it remember I am a Christian now stronger than ever we don't do witches the bible says suffer not a witch to live. In other words they burn them on the stake. So crying out to God he gave me a scripture psalms 18. And it was talking about protections and that my enemy was too strong for me but God himself was going to fight my enemy for me. So I believe every word of psalms and comfort came to me and I got up and knock on her door and made conversation with her. I plainly ask her if she was indeed a witch and she said yes she was but she was not praticing it anymore because a friend of hers died do to the fact of a spell that was cast upon him from other witches and I thought really.

Well I do not know what I did but for a short while she like me. I bought her all new clothes no black and I took her to the salon and did her hair a few times. Now by this time there is no fear of defeat I am feeling matter of fact I know that I have the power greater that she. So bobby tells her that her vacation is over and that she has to help out around here and that he would assign her chores. little did he or I know that she was very lazy. So he told her 20 a week she will get for helping out he told her he wanted the kitchen clean but I did not want her cleaning my kitchen because I did not feel that she would do a job to my standards any how. so he took us fishing my son came home for school break and we all went fishing and bobby and her got into and she stood toe to toe with him and he was surprise and so was I and he warn her and told her that he would not put his hands on her cause he was not going to jail but at the same time if you do not abide by my rules you have to go. So things quiet down and they had their moment when they did not share too many words with each other and he then told her I do not want that witch stuff coming to this house. So I took her to sars and coble book store on an outing of ours and she order a black magic book that I did not know about and she talk with the clerk she knew the book by name and they was out of the book and she had them order the book. But I did not know at the time that the book order was a black magic book but I did know that she order a book. well a week later on her allowance day Friday the store call and said that her book was in and bobby answer the phone from the call from the store clerk about the book being in and he was reviewing her chores status evaluation of her weekly performances and he said that she would not recieve the allowance because her performance was terrible that he did not see where she did any work at all..So she was furious because they call and said that the book had arrive and she wanted this black magic book. So she curse him out and he said that is it you cannot stay here you have to go because you will make me put my hands on you and I am not going to jail. So he packed her bags and moved her out on the spot. I was rejoicing in my heart because God proved his Word to me when he gave psalms 18 that my enemy was too many and too strong for me and for me to step back because he would handle it. Now just a quick review and a few pointers I left out. The voodoo doll that fell out of the car from her when she was 8, then all the head and sickness that I constant had during the time she came to visit. She told me a story how she herself had dramatic head pains and health issues it happen to her suddenly she shared with me I ask her when then it occur and people it was the same time I fell on my knees and prayed to send this affliction back to the sender in the name of Jesus. And mind you when I prayed it, it was too the dark world the devil I had no person in mind when I prayed it. When she stood in my kitchen telling me her health attacks I knew right then and there that she was the one sending the affliction to me. She came to destroy and to divide and to conquer. She spoke to me that you know my father's lover is around the corner and he frequently is over there he also took me to meet her since I been at your house. I believe that Bobby knew that she was going to reveal that info to me but what he did not know is that she reveal it early on and I heard it but was not sure if she was speaking the truth because I could not understand why she would share it with me. So soon after her departing Bobby departed as well. And sure enough he went to the lady house around the corner from me. Years ago when Bobby would drop and pick up my granddaughter from school her discover one of his old high school girlfriends was my daughter teacher. And they connected again and he would bribe my granddaughter not to tell by giving her anything she wanted from the store and I could never understood it until know. This was the same woman that my daughter calls me and told me that she would see in my car. Daily... During this season in my life I was growing greater in my faith and I was in a zone all by myself. As I went deeper into the studies of God my world around me was crumbling. My business my clients were decreasing. My family was so distance from me you would have thought that I had no family at all. I lost everything around me. I found myself one-step away from homeless. God provided and I had just enough to sustain me. I live with no lights or gas for time to time. I would either have gas on or lights on and this went on for three years. No car on public transportation. And now facing to be unemployed because the death of the owner. I was made fun of mock talk about in and out of church. But God allow me to become owner of the business and supernatural in one month's time I was back on my feet with a new focus or new project being a salon owner it was exciting. But that was all that was going on good, still I had enough to guarantee me work but still not above my needs and wants I was just afloat. The new stylist that works at the salon was great people some great good people and some great bad people. They help my life to be exciting but. I found myself in a women support group and out of the group it was all broken women from bad relationships with men as somehow we came together and perform a city wide march on sexual immorality. and this was the time when the down low men story was coming out so we had the march and it was so powerful and so informative to us and others and we became sisters in the support group from our church. We all went to the same church. I do not know why I share so much about bobby and I but this was the first time I found out who I was it was a time when I was in great separation f the worlds and a time of self reflection for me. There was a time when our church took the entire church out in the community to witness to people on the street about Jesus. And at this time I was over a department in my church call the evangelist department. And I was directed by my pastor to demonstrate what the department does and involve them by allowing them to have and see hands on training. Now this was on a Sunday afternoon now my pastor picks the location that we would go in, which was the same area and street that Bobby and his mistress live on and I thought wow. Silence that I was I just said Lord you know only you know. Now my church never knew bobby because he did not come to church with me he had nothing to do with it. So as we arrive we divided the people in groups and I thought good I will not have to be the one that knocks on the door where Bobby is and so far so good we about to finish the demonstration and my Pastor calls me over and tell me to train the people that is on the porch where Bobby is at and I could have fainted and so we knock but no one came to the and I said thank you Lord for not being embarrass but know I see the so the good Lord saved my face that day. So one Sunday I was ask to come to the front of the church by my pastor and he said to me tell your husband that the Lord said if he do not get his life together he will face danger. Now while we had been separated I never shared with my pastor that my husband had left me. The church thought he was just a husband that did not attend church. But leaving church that day I passed him by on the road for the first time and I had not seen him in a while. And I thought how interesting I get this word for him today and I run into him I saw him but he did not see me. so months pass by and one cold December night I get a call from his sister and he had three but they never call me and it was his younger sister and she said bobby has been stab and you have to come to the hospital and I said ok. but I hung the phone up and I continue to do hair trying to decide if I were going at all but I knew that I would finish my client and then I will go if I go. so I get to the hospital and they were releasing him and they ask could he come to my house and I though really I have not seen you in two or three years and just like that you come back to my house and I figure it out that he did not have a place to go to and that is why they call me. I let this man my house and he was stabbed multiple times and he had urine and fetsis on him and he ask me to clean him and I was so hesitant to do it and he knew it but I did it. In his recovery there were detectives that came by and when I ask what had happen he would not tell me and also he would not let me go to court with him or be in the room when police question him. Well folks the story was his mistress sons ambush and stabbed him multiple times he was doing their mom wrong more than likely. so the mistress call his sister to call him to tell him that she missed him and that her sons was no longer living with her and she wanted him to come back. Yes I heard the sister tell him this. Well the following week I came home from work and this man was gone I had a Dear John letter and he left. Yap this is the truth folks he was at my house a total of 30 days..I felt use and abuse and so stupid. But at this time I was poison in my mind and heart because the worse he treated me the more I was addicted to him. I was in love with God and in love with him.4 months past and I was recovering in my pain from his betrayal to me but all that I had been through it was over ten years it was finally his turn for the storm to hit his house.. His sister first born child very young died and it hit the family very hard and 30 days later his youngest sister first born child died and weeks later less than three his father was in a comma and eventually died. His mistress uncle or cousin died as well in less than 45 days. And one of his sisters told him you need to go back to your wife and get your life in order because God must be speaking to this family. So I ask him when I heard of the first death can I go to the funeral and he told me no because his mistress would be there and I did not go but I brought flowers and plants to the sister house and not knowing that he and his mistress was there along with his entire family. I left and later they plan two more funerals 2 nephews 1 father and 1 brother in law. These women had embrace bobby and his mistress they celebrated ever holiday with his sisters and mom and the ironic thing was they all experience the lost of their husband and sons. March 2my phone rings and he is on the phone very humble can I come home please and I thought no please no I want to be divorce Lord I want a new husband. So when I got home that day he was in my home he used his key from years ago. I did not change the locks because he never threatened to come back. I did not know what was his mind or heart and it was a strange encounter. Well we moved and tried to begin again. He enrolled in school and I was engulf in ministry and we were pleasant to each other for a while we both were busy. I continue in city marches Jesus walks Christians rights movements television and radio interviews all the time. And I just thought I will wait on the Lord concerning this marriage. I think that one quality I have to give Bobby credit for is that he never stood in the way of my relationship with the Lord and he supported me by helping if I needed it. I had complete freedom in that area. But the journey finally came to an end in 2007. The beginning of the year the lady he had an affair with on the job that the union brought a child a girl. She would be seven years old at this time the mother calls and says she wants bobby to be in the child life and she was ready to let him see her. And I was so jealous because we had no children together and children were out of the question for us. Bobby wanted his first visit to be alone in meeting them and I thought that no way I am your wife we do this together. But it did not happen and I felt on the outside again and when will I be in the front or on this man side the way a wife suppose to be. I thought this time I will brace myself and prepare myself for his let down and I fear this reunion between them because he husband just died and they might get together again. So bobby pulled away from me. I never met the child and things just was not right and Bobby told me I am not your husband your husband is in church but I am not your husband, little did I know that while he was saying this his bags were already pack. It was psalm Sunday in April and I knew that something different was going to happen.

Palms Sunday I prayed this prayer Lord help me accept the changes in my life that I do not want to face. Help me Lord to be strong and to release this man. He has released me but I truly have not released him. I remember one day walking up the stairs and hearing a conversation bobby was having with his cousin, his cousin told him to leave the mistress alone and do your wife right and bobby told his cousin I will never let her go I will keep her and my wife the both. I heard this and I shook my keys to let him know I was coming up and I shook my keys to let him know that I was coming up the stairs of our house. He dismisses himself from the conversation with his cousin. I took my church cloths off and handed him over the keys to the car because that was procedure you see I drove the new car because it was mines and he drove the old beat up jeep that I had bought for him the second year in our marriage. Well he left to go to his mistress house as usual which he would always tell me that he was going to watch the game with the fellows and he could not bring the fellows to the house because I was to religious for them and I would not say anything because I value my quiet times on Sundays after church to just replay my good time in the house of the Lord. Now on this particular Palm Sunday after

I prayed the prayer to be courageous and accept bobby being not the one for me. Just let me take you to how the day began that morning he came in from work and he wanted to take me to church and I did not want to be dropped off and we argued and we were already the both of us to the boiling pot point because before he went into to work the mother of his child call to get specifics on their meeting and I did not like how that went down because he was excited and I was really left out so I had great fear what if he fall in love with her again or she fall in love with him. She gave him a child I could not give him one. So when he went to work he left on a bad note. That morning when he came in the one thing he said to me that he was not my husband and never was and my husband is at the church I go to but he was the wrong guy for me. He knew when ever he said that, that would get me very heated and angry. So going to church he had warned me that when I got back that it may very well be a Dear John letter for me because he was very good at those kind of letters since I had received countless numbers of them before from him. The service was very unusual very short and I ask God in prayer to give me the strength to face and handle anything that bobby had plan for me that day. I linger around the church and I finally went toward home because that was my Sunday routine come straight home and release the car to him. But as I was driving I decided to go down his mistress street I would get to her house before I get to mine and so I did I came up through the back way and driving very slowly there was no traffic on the road. I notice a man and a dog and that man was bobby he did not see me but I saw him and he was coming toward me and then spotted me and turns around to go into his mistress house. But I step on the gas pedal and their I went he ran through her door and I pulled up onto her grass and I said to him that I was not leaving until he comes out very loud and putting all their business out their. So then he stuck his head out of the upstairs window and said leave please. We began to have a conversation through her window he explain that his connection there was just his dog that she allow to stay there after their break up I said oh really. I said come home with me right now. H e said no you go and I will be there. I told him if you do not leave with me know and let me drive off without you can forget it I am done. I know he did not believe me I had been saying things like this for the entire 12 years of the marriage. So I left and went home and went to the closet to put his stuff out and low and behold he had luggage secretly pack to leave anyway. He had already plan to leave me so I put the bags on the porch and while doing so he pulls up in friend car and gets out and I tell him that he will not be staying here any longer that I was done all kinds of flash back entering my mind while I sitting his stuff out. Things like driving and running into him and her and his explanation oh she needed a ride from work and she help me so many I could go on and on and another one when I ran into him he seen me first and I had some mail of his this was before he came back and when I caught up with him she was in the car the police was call because they said I tried to run them off the road which I did not and the officer took me to jail that day. The officer said which one is your wife he told them that his mistress was because he had been with her longer than with me. But back to the event of me getting strength to put old boy out. While things were happing at my house a couple from the church happen to drive by and see the confrontation between us and said that they were going to stay until they see I was alright and he went in the back and started up that old jeep that I thought was not running or broke for the last year to find out that it was just an lie to keep me at home so I would not run into him and his mistress anymore. Bobby started the jeep up and his words to me that day was I do not love you I love her and good you saw and do not bother us ever again you are not my wife she is! I watch him drive off and lock my house up and went with the couple from my church for a few hours.

What oh no? You mean not butterflies in my stomach? You mean anxiety attacks or oppression and depression or despair. I could not believe I never experience this long time without these feelings occurring that is why I did not want to let go because I did not want to go through that emotional roller coaster ride. Besides I hate rollercoasters. The fourth in the year and I had lost the location of my business and had to move business in the basement of my home, I had the betrayal of close friend whom I consider a best friend that took the business location from me. She my friend sublease from me but had intensions of getting out of her lease from me and being the main lease holder once my lease was up for renewal an agreement was made between the building owner and her not to renew my lease and give her the contract instead. Yes did happen while a citywide major project was going involving the church I attended that I was put head event planner and was sat down from all church duties at the church I attended lastly but not lease my present landlord brought me to court for evictions slow payments partials all this in a span of three months I think oh a suspended license for not having proof of insurance and falling to go to court simply because I forgot because so much was happening to me. But audience in spite of all this humiliation I kept my head up I continue to go to the church and smile. I said when I look back over my life and see what The Good Lord has done for me and brought me through I learn to be at peace and took advantage to be with my grinds and daughter because I was always busy doing me!, So I went back to being a booth renter instead of salon owner and I tell you folks not long and I do mean not long. I was coming from another church service and I got a call on my cell phone from a brother in my church saying that he had heard from God in a vision and the vision he saw was that I was to be his bride. Now he shared this short message with me and I was stunned and did not know what to say but ok brother I will get back with you. I continue to drive home and laugh and fell asleep and did not wake up until the next day.

I remember telling it to 2 friends of mines at least I thought they were but they was far from being my friends these two were the ones that had schema against to take the building from me which I may say they were very successful. So they share it with all at the church which I did not know at that time. But it did not matter because what God have for you is for you and no devil or demon from hell can stop the plan of God over someone life. I had grew distance from all my siblings I do not know why but it was a mutual departure we was not nasty or angry with one another but there was not that bond. Some it had to do with my father they said favour me and they did not let it go. So they all stayed close like we was raise but I was cast out just to make things plain. So going through this back stabbing season of betrayal I did not or could not pick up the phone and call the sisters because I had similar vibes coming from them. So what happen that maybe should not or should have I am not sure is the brother from church became my leaning post aside from God. We talk almost every night and I tell you thanks to him it kept my mind in one piece. I told him thank you for talking to me you don't know how much this means to me. He thought I was just being friendly and kind but I knew God had him there in my life to keep me sane because the devil tried to wipe me out but I tell through all this my spirit was uplift and encourage I started going to the track and working out and just exhaling and inhaling the fresh early morning air and the fellowship of the people that was in or apart of the community. I went to that track sometimes and most times twice a daily even on Sunday's wow. Walking around the track and talking to him while walking losing weight and eating healthy. Now I was excited about being divorce from bobby. I thought to be married to a church man a saved man wow I never had that. That would be very interesting and I would like that no drama when it come to honoring the marriage. So I proceeded with the divorce and it seem like it was not moving fast enough for me. It was a wrench in the process I needed to find or locate bobby and get him to sign and release me and I though oh no I do not even want to think about it, but I went forward and contacted him to sign the paper so he came to me and sign the paper and he did something that I did not expect he began to cry and to tell me that he love me and will all ways love me and then he said that I was in love with the church and did not treat him with the same honour I gave to the church. Then he said you lost all this weight baby you look good why did you not look this good for me. and I was silent and he said I am moving down south and when I get myself together I am going to send for you and we will try it again you watch and see and he cry and then I cried because we both knew that it was truly good bye. He hug me no kisses and left. and I shut the door and I had two emotions going on I was sad because it was real that day when he sign the divorce papers and it was joy because I had something or someone to look forward to. I guess you are wondering, I told brother jay I would married him and I though I was in a hurry he was on speed dial. so phoning I told him that I got the paper sign he asks me how much did I owe on my divorce and I told him and he ran the money over to me to pay the lawyer off because I was on a payment plan because my finances had been cut tremendously. Oh I forgot to mentioned that I was doing the sister hair in my basement. This was the one that stop by the day I put bobby out and she knew the details to our situation and she knew brother jay at the church and I told her that I was unsure about jays vision about me being his wife and she share how he was a nice man and I was concern about the what the people at church would say seeing I got a Proposal and I am legally still married on paper. And her remark was favour ain't fair. But after she left I ask him could I come and see where he live and how he lived and he said sure and people when I got there his house was dark and thousand of papers on everywhere and neglect from front to the back. I was not impressed. He like me had been married twice all his children by his first wife they have 5 together and his second marriage no children together but about 7 stepchildren. child support eating him up and at this point I was drawn to the man over the phone but not the man in person because immediately I am thinking he can be a burden needy I do not want to be desperate for love that I will stoop down and accept anything and I walk away saying just pause it girl slow down take your time you do not want to be so vulnerable that you find yourself in a bind. So I was struggling and I thought I once told this young lady if God told you to married this guy on our job would you marry him and she replied no I would not and I reinstated to her but if God. But God told you to marry him would you and she said even if God said to I would not and I thought you silly woman. If God told you best believe feeling it or not I would do it whatever the purpose would be do it. So in that moment I remember my thoughts on our conversation and I prayed again out loud God if this is you and you told me to live in a garbage can with this fellow I will God but I have to know this is you. And instantly I felt this overwhelming comforting and this burst of anticipation so much so that I had to take a seat. Then the phone rang and it was him calling me on his break at work and was instantly intrigue and amazed and flatter and not ashamed but thinking this is it finally I will get what I expect to get from a man in a relationship. So this is where we meet up and we both are on speed dial as to say I am in just a hurry as he is. What I like about him is that he knew what he wanted and did not have to get other opinions concerning it. I was not taken around his family or friends for an approval he said the Lord should me you and that settles it. Now opposite of Bobby he wore the Elvis Presley suede shoes with fur on it when we got married and that was a tell sign that he was a ladies' man. But here on the other hand Brother Jay wore the pat boon vanilla shoes that needed replenishing and I thought this man needs help! So I began to help him with his makeover and his first change of apparel and groom appearance I said wow. He literally went to church and had entire audience surrounding him because of his transformation. I thought listen my divorce is still processing and I cannot make you a centrepiece just yet. So took him to me my eldest son that at the time live maybe 23 miles or 30 away from the city and we met briefly with him and my daughter in-law and was anxious to have time for ourselves so heading back to the city we stop and looked at some model home in the sub that son lived in and Jay and I tour the model home fully furnished and he took the gentleman card that was handling the cell of the house. And I thought nothing of it I was happy to live in a nice affordable apartment in the city just to start new that is all that I was concern about. One lady from church said her husband heard the women at the church saying how does Liz get a marriage proposal and she is still married and we single and waiting. I knew from this statement that anything and everything had been spoken about us some good but mostly evil. so a week exactly from seeing the house the real-estate man calls Jay and they presue purchasing the house and the guy said he need a lease a grand down to even consider it. And jay gave him a post dated check a iou check to hold and the man took it. And so many people were looking at the house and the guy told him that he wanted him to get the house and that he was not going to accept any other offers now only you got to get approve for it. So we drove back out to the house and if ask me if I wanted it and I said yes but we do not have to reach so hig because honestly I do not have the faith for it is beyond our dreams. His question was again give me a yea or no if you want it and I said yes and he said pray and agree with me right here that the Lord will make away and open doors that we can get it so I said ok. He took the holy oil out of his pocket and pour it on the ground of the property and he prayed and I agree with him. We drove of and driving off he and I said I do not know about you but I feel rich and I said I do too. So the realtor refer and wonderful oriental young man that work mortgages loans applications on the side he had many trades going on and he put him on our case and for 30 to no more than 45 or less we were back and forth qualifying and so many turn downs and stipulations and the owner need to sell within thirty days and we talking about close to three hundred thou-sand home. I could offer no help we were marry yet and I did have nothing to bring to the table but my agreement and support. Jiggle jangle upside down and turn around we was spinning when even the people said maybe it just not meant to be Jay it is meant to be and we will be in the home and wow he had everyone involve pulling for him at that point. Then the call came we were approve and on target within the period of time we had a closing date. This may Jay had a ram in the bush he had a saving put way that Lord had preserve for him in his 401k and was able to draw a large sum to it out and put it on the down payment.

Now the house went through and a matter of days for closing and when the date of the closing Jay hands me the keys to the fully furnish house a and tells me to stay in it. And that he will move in when we get married so I get my bags because that is all I could bring because his things and my things were consider garbage to bring. The scenery was as beautiful as the presidential suites.

Wow is not the words for this house. I went from rags to riches. Then slam wham. The church said that they would not marry us. That it was so many issues going on in our lives and they felt we needed to wait awhile and I thought wow this man will obey what the church tells him and if they decide their will be no marriage then he would respect the decision. So waiting in this grand house to see if there will be a wedding I decided to go forward in my preparations and seek a wedding dress. friend and I went very early in the morning to the bridal shop and on our journey their we stop at my daughter house, for what I cannot remember right now but after we left my daughter house we get a call to turn around and come back because the cops were at her house to take her to jail because her 10 year old daughter ran to friends house and told them that my daughter had spank her. And they did they call the police and when I arrive back to my daughter house the police was there hand cuffing her and taking her to jail because it was said that she hit her child on the arm which the child was not hit but grabbed and told to go to her room and stay out of adult conversations. My grandchild was embraced and mad because others witness it. So now I have to stop what was going with and be a granny and handle the family business. Well this thing escalated and my daughter was in jail for two weeks she lost her job and was put on probation and was not allow to see her child for 30 days. Wow how strange that was the first time my grand child was chastised. She never had a whipping before ever in life. So officials force me to take the child out of the house because my daughter was returning home. Now my grandchild who lied to authorities has to come and stay with me inlay home and I am not sure if there will be a wedding. Yeah right! So before I can get my feet in the door I am coming in with issues. School arrangements the whole nine yards I am operating in while being on pins and needles. So yeah I have my divorce papers in my hand and call jay with some good news and jay goes to the pastor and ask him will you marry us. Now jay wanted a wedding but I did not I just want to be married no wedding and the pastor was embarass to perform the wedding because of all the talk that was going on. So we had two marriage counselling sessions and still no approval if we would-be married and finally the answer came and we was told that the church could not perform the wedding. Then I did not give jay any slack and I ask him are you going to do what God told you or the church. But no response for Jay just a look of despair............but because jay was so respectful to the Man of God and was humble when he heard the decision. Jay went and fell on his knees and the church mothers grabbed him and prayed and before they all could get up from their knees the ll called and said ok I will married you in my office Wednesday. And between going to court and having child protective interviewing and trying to prepare for a wedding I was worn out and he was and I went to target and found something and he was casual and one deacon came in to be a witness while the Wednesday night bible study was going on. We said I do and gave each other a smack on the lips nothing long because I was so nervous I was shaking in my boots. And I was nervous of the pastor that performs the wedding since he had mix feeling about marrying us. So jay took me to meet his mother that night and we stay there a good while and when we got to the house because it was such a long ride. We both was so wore out I would like to say that the wedding began the next day.

All things were so beautiful and new. And know now my new life begins with dreams and visions that I had kept in my heart to married to a God fearing man. We did not know each other so there.

Were many times we step on each other toes as if we both were learning how to learn the two step dance for the first time. I never calculated that I was not just marrying him but his dreams and visions as well. Not knowing that we would often have a show down as to who dreams and visions would be put first. Yes I must admit that I thought that my dreams which was of ministry full time and world travel would not be a problem because we both saved right? It should not be a problem. I also believed that I would have a church to preach the gospel. It was not sure about pasturing a church but certainly preaching in the church. There is a difference between the two. This was an issue because although my husband is saved and been in the church faithful and for many years even longer than I he did not or do not believe in woman pastors at all the end of story. So I'm thinking wow my life will be on hold again and the dreadful waiting again. Wow when will my life begin or start and will it ever.? Then everything that I had walked into suddenly did not mean a hill of beans to me. Because it is another fellow that is not sensitive to my desires I am connected to again. And here now here comes his family, the love of his life his children whom he is deeply connected to more than I ever seen in a man in my life. His bond was and is so strong for his children. He immediately wanted me to had the same affection for his children that he had and being the honest person that I am I told him that honey this will take time and we need to developed and learn each other first. I think that after the wedding and out with our pastor, our pastor ask him if he thought that we would have a child together and he responded that oh no I do not want any children all my children are by one woman. Then the pastor said well you may reconsider I think it would be good if you to have a child together if would bond you to closer and it would be good. And he again responded oh no. And I tell you that I was very disappointed and upset by his respond and I kept those remarks hidden in my heart. I felt that if I was the woman that you were going to spend the rest of your life with and God himself show you and told you that I was your wife why wouldn't you want something to express our love together in the result of a child. I was so puzzle about that. Now I was old 47 at the time and he 44 and I knew that I was pass the child bearing age but to me it is a sign of love when a man ask a woman to have his baby for her. That woman is honoured but if a man says that he doesn't want a child by a woman that woman is very dishonoured. That is just the way I feel. And that day a door in my heart shut towards him and he knew it not right at the start line of our marriage...So when he would make a statement to me like anyone who doesn't love my children like they love me I do not want to be bother with them. And I would say well I am your wife and I am not there mom they have a mother whom they all are very close to and my role is not to try and take her role, I am your wife only. And I know it was showing through that I was not being open to the mother or stepmom role for his children. I thought if I do not ask or expect you to be my children father particular my grandchildren because all my children were grown during this time then he should let it go and let me be his wife as he stated that he did not want us to bare children together. So our sit down dinner time with his family he discover some personnel belongings to us had been gone into and he discover it not I and I was not accustom to my belonging being going into and I became furious and I told him that I was not confront able with his family coming over to visit again and this was a great blow up with us he and his kids against me. And let me say for the record never did I have a verbal disagreement with the children or them with me but my husband and I would have these arguments about the kids between only the two of us. So now I got my husband feeling uncomfortable in his own home which I can say I do greatly regret today. So quest what this behaviour tore us apart with the only common thing we had together was the love of the church. The arguments had got so bad that all the people at the church was talking about our marriage and I would be so embarrass to the point that I did not want to go and every one there was my enemy and I could not demonstrate the love I preached about at all. Then my husband would not make it any better he would purposely humiliate me and shared things that should stay in your house and not with outsiders. And he would not stop because I believe in his mind he felt like I married this Witch she is controlling she does not like my children or my family. She thinks she is better than them. She forgot where she came from. I bought this house so I can enjoy it everybody is welcome to my house. Now that is what he would say to me and people he wanted to expose me to. But he was just as quilt as I was because but he was just as guilty as me because his hospitality was not very welcoming from those that were quest of mines. And just let me make it clear that he would not be rude but he would excuse his self in a way that all would know that he was not engaging or inviting so they stay would be very short. So my children live very near to us but I would see them only on holidays to our house but when I wanted to see them I would go to their house to visit them. And when his children and he would talk which would be daily he would step out of the room or sit in the car while talking and most calls would be exchange during his time of working hours. Now I am thinking did not get into this marriage for this. This point in my life or our life we she should be experiencing family and sharing and giving back in life to family and friends. Their once was when I was on this journey to give back seeing that we were bless by having a nice home and all our kids were doing ok that I tried to convince him to let do foster care and take in some children or one child to give back. During this time a lot of churches was having a program and giving ads about it and I made several calls and went to the foster care centre, But I could not get my husband to jump on board with that idea and then I was tire of the division in our home and I suggested that maybe his girls could come and stay with us and he said they said know that our household was a bit strict and they was not ready to live under those conditions. So I am thinking I want to be comfortable and I want to be able to take any of my children in if they need me butt appears to be ours house and not our children home if they need it. Now strong thoughts are coming to me that I was trick the is not my husband I need to be with my first husband yes I went all the Way back to my first husband. I thought he and I would be available for our children and grandchildren needs and we would not have to be bother with acceptance or permission if or when a crisis was there concerning them. I knew that my children and their father had developed a great relationship and he was very much involve in their lives. And I kept thinking wow this divorce thing is not cool I see why God did not like it because of so many factors down the road that we as individuals don't consider. For instance my daughter had a baby and needed desperate she needed shelter for her and children and when she came out of the hospital to our house from having the baby I was so nervous of the children running and breaking things or touching things that I made her so ncomfortable that she would not stay because I felt I would get them before he would-be upset. And I thought now if this was her dad it would be no issue because these are his grandchildren. So things like that folks were plaguing mind constantly. Some times I welcome the thoughts and often times I would fight the thoughts depending upon if we argue or not that they. Then I began to realize that I was sinning in my heart according to the bible and our belief because the bible says in it if a man or woman lust or desire in their heart for anyone that persons is committing adultery in their heart. So that itself would cause me to be fearful because did not want to sin and suffer the punishment. Also thoughts of you know Liz your sin when you married this man you know you was not legally release and you was married while dating this man. Yeah this cannot be your husband God does not do things in this order. Quit trying to make your sin fit with excuses God word does not change. I would say often to my husband you know I or we sin this is not God this marriage there is no proof that his is God look at our lives the disconnection of the family God is all about unity and family. I would ask him don't you feel this way also. His respond would be every time Liz you are my wife I know what God told me and showed me and often I would get angry at his response I would say that he is doing this to torment me. I thought Oh God if it was not for our love that you and I have together I would leave but inspire of everything that my husband and I was encountering in our marriage God was still moving us forward and we were growing I would like to call it we were going through growing pains. You see in spite of those that were talking about us there were those that did not know our business and thought wow they are bless. Wow she has a real Cinderella story or in the bible an Esther story that she is in the king's palace. You see God will hide and cover our filth and dirt and he would be the one that chasten us. We suffer 3 accidents or within 4 years one Sunday Gods mercy was upon our lives daily we argue every time we were in the car together. Because I battle with of driving the highways and some large avenues and I would feel that when we would have to go places he would express his anger toward me through his driving abilities. And this was an absolute mess that would occur in the car while driving. I would become child like with emotions of fear and there would be no remedy or mercy but to get out and the more I express my fear was the more he would terrorized me in the driving. And this causes me to resent him very deeply. Because his number one role to me was protection and safety and he was on the opposite side of his role. When we got married I told him all my weakness and fears and he was not sensitive to me concerning them. We move very far away from the church and his job and connections and I needed to ride with him to Acomplish ministry needs and emergency needs because of my driving issues and he just appear to show unkindness and put me in the position of begging or humility just to ride. So one day he was arguing and he got loud while driving and when he does that I will pull back and let him know that ok you won now stop driving mad because I am there I am scared you have achieve but this time it was to late not paying attention he was not he drove through the green light but there was another car coming running the light I scream stop the car is coming he tried to speed up to get out they way and they hit us and he drove into a telephone pole hitting me on the passenger side meanwhile they hit him on the driver side my head went through the windshield air bags going off van is total it was brand new not even 2 months old just got it off the lot. We got out and the drivers ran and when we got home my son came and got us we got check out by ambulance neither of us knew how badly we both was injure at that time but when we made it to the house my husband Jay pass out I did not know it at the time but my son and him was outside side and he collapse onto the ground. My son then told me call ambulance he is out we put blankets around him my son begin to pray and call on the Lord and speak life to him I was historical and all negative emotions about him went out of the window and I knew I would be lost without him and that I love him. You see people you can fight and argue so much that you cannot see that you love each other and you really do not know why your are disagreeing so much and fighting so much. Bottom line is we fought each other to keep from getting hurt by each other that is crazy I know and the enemy will have you do crazy things that do not make sense. So hi is hospitalize and I did not get care or check out I went home that night and they kept him several days and I was not able to move to walk and from my head to my feet. And when he came home oh we appreciated.

Each other for a while but as soon as the healing came we went back to the fighting. But I fought less because I understood that it was a warning no doubt and God was grieve that we both behave that way especially representing him. I told my and that we have to be careful and that we was warned but my husband denied it he said that did not have nothing to do with God and I said ok you can believe that it did not but i believe different. Then another time arguing he leaves and I told him not and bam! another accident. He wasn't hurt but if was as if i was saying i will get out of his way because I do not want him to suffer because of me so this journey help me to turn the other cheek and avoid arguments so much more. God was training me to be submitted and I did need to defend myself but he would do it for me just God wanted me to do the right thing even if unfairness and injustice was rendered to me. So maybe a year to the date another accident with my husband had occurred he in the car by his self and again pass out and was taken to hospital in ambulance the same identical way only this time the driver stayed and did not leave the scene but he was in the right they in the wrong but him the exact place and when I rush to hospital and he was in some discomfort I look at him as to say we know God did not do this and he does not do things like this but when you are out of the will of God you are an open target for the enemy to attack you. So my journey was I got to-do my part to help him make it in.

So busy going to my salon or my private suite I take off and begin to engulf myself in my job, because it is a public place and I get to be received and accepted by clients. Working kept me sane. It would give me the strength to battle the atmosphere at home. The more my husband became angered and it seems as miserable with life. I grew more and more compassion because I realized that he was being tormented and there was to me a jealousy spirit and a comparison spirit he displays to me and often when I would address it he of course would deny it. I t appear that my husband worked very hard not just on his job but in the church and most tome labor at the church harder than at his job. I was going to say at his paying job but the church was his paying job as well because all his sibling are still living his mom and dad his children all employed and in school none on the street and no bad news and we did have saving but we chose both of us to give what we had to missions, in and out the states honestly I worked and render my entire pay to missions weekly and he did large portion as well but he paid all the bills and I bought groceries and things needed in the house. But our problem was even though we were together he sometimes felt that we I would get bless or a good report he did not look at that this was our blessing or this family blessing we had arguments over who would get the credit for the blessing the faithful labor in church yeah or the giving to missions I know sad right? But these things do occur unfortunately. Oh how do I deal with this kind of partner I thought. So when I figure out do not try to figure him out get to know you. I tell you that working on self was so humbling. I learn so much about me and that I was not all that. And discovering how mess up I was I thought oh my goodness Lord I cannot think of anybody on this earth that I could live with and be comfortable that can deal with my issues all my imperfections, Lord there is no one but Jay that does not mind how I look the personal issues like the fear concerning driving. Oh I forgot to mention he have a slight handicap and that is he has no sense of direction so I knew my direction and he would always want me to go with him because he had no direction. So people would tell us that we made a great pair together people he could go to a place several and never learn how to get there again is case was pretty bad. But I begin to be very thankful because I realize that we both were mess up and I was thankful that he put up with me. And he was right I could not see it but I did think that I was better but I was blind to myself I did not know that I was selfish you see I could justify all my behaviors and give reasons why but that doesn't excuse the fact that when you mess up and you are not right your are not right. When I became to be so thankful of God's grace and love and his mercy for me I was humble and somewhat shame and I said God you put up with me with all mess and you gave others a heart to tolerate me in all my evil. Lord please forgive me I am no better than no one. I realize that my husband was giving me back to me and indeed this was not him his reactions towards me but me. He was truly frustrated because the woman he was told to marry is not the woman that he have. So I realize I hurt him and his feeling are important. His children me and the whole wide world to him and in the beginning of the relationship I hit him below the belt because made it clear that I was not they mama I was his wife and I knew that he would receive it as rejection and well as me receiving from him rejection when he stated that he only wanted his children by the mother of his children and that response from him was received as rejection from his part to me. Now daily I find myself daily in everthing telling the Good Lord thank you for my life, my husband because is in this marriage for the long haul. He told me that he will never divorce me or leave me he don't do that the wives he had before me they left the marriage he did not he is committed in the bad as well as the good. So I am appreciated I am in a place in my life where it do not matter who is right or wrong in marriage as well as outside of marriage all relationships. I want to show peace I am changing I found out that it is important to see how others see me as well and others can help me see myself because what counts is how I respond and deliver myself in life to others. Now that God has got me to this place I can and am mature enough for him to trust me with his treasures from heaven. Now the dream is now being fulfilled in my life I am no longer saying ok Lord you bless with this but what about that Lord. Or Lord this blessing is good but that thing is so bad that I cannot even enjoy the blessing you gave me. Wait a minute something is wrong with this picture the bible says that the blessing of the Lord added rich and has no sorrow and it seems like every blessing that I get it was sorrow with it. Wisdom tells me that I know God does not make mistakes so it must be me that is doing something wrong not God being mean to me. Lord you really is completing the work you began in me huh. Who would have told me that at 54 years I was ready to be His showcase trophy? That we have completed 7 years of marriage and if I can explain it there is a weight lifted upernatural. We know that we stood the test and the Good Lord must have said to Satan enough is enough leave them alone flee! I tell you the truth it like I have awaken from a dream instantly restoration was granted it was mutual we look at each other and there was a gaze in both our eyes that had not been there since the first few months of marriage. I must have repented for everything I done in every relationship I ever had even when I was not old or big enough to ride a bike and I am sure he did as well. He showed me that I was his responsibility and I liked that very much. Expressed of disagreements but no arguments, while we have arrive. I knew that we were living or having the marriage the bible says we are to have and I would not or could not accept anything less than that. I heard so many times well this is life and you will find the perfect marriage or family and that may be true but I have had the privilege of meeting couples that did not take one another down and so seeing that from others testimony I knew it was achievable and to God be the Glory he allowed me to now experience it. Look I will take it at any part of my life I am grateful. Now things are lining up and I have no reason to fear because I trust him now because I had and trust issue with God I know he has my destiny in his plans. So ministry is calling the both of us and there is no more jealousy or competition and we are listening and hearing each other heart. That is something that we both was guilty of I complain the entire marriage he doesn't listen and all the time I did not listen to his heart. Well people I have had the prescience of God Holy Spirit so close to me that has been lingering daily and this never happen before like this. There is just blessing lying down and waking up. Thank you Lord. So I believe that this is my hour that he is sending us out to preach his word. The scriptures have open up to me with so much clarity and understanding it is as if I am seeing through his eyes and wisdom knowledge and understanding is present. My husband is telling me he is proud of what God is doing in my life and I am telling him the same. We both asked to preach and both did quite well with the help of the Holy Spirit being present. And quests what he gave our first time being the main speakers a deliverance and word of knowledge, this is a good sign that he the Lord is the Potter and we are his clay and he fashion us to his desire and I am please that I am in the Masters hand and he is touching us. My advice is that I could have been here so much sooner if I had only believe and watched the words that allow to proceed out of my mouths that did not bring me joy and strength but the words that I spoke kept me in fear and depress. No matter what you got to say what he says about you no matter what.. So he visited me and met me in my house this year and doing my routine daily duties no expecting him to come and show up with his presence and revealing his self powerful in his word to me and when I discover that there is a shift something is different about this prayer time this reading time it was like I was reading it for the first time I pause several times in total amazements wondering really you are truly revealing your mysteries to little old me really? and it would two to three days before sometimes I would go back to the word because what he showed me would be such and revelation I would go over and over in my head what was just reveal and I could not go further until he was willing to release me and it became that all that I would revelation would be ongoing as reading the scriptures. And like never before I would get daily visit in person on phone calls daily with counseling someone and in all the counseling there would be encouraging with everyone. And I would be exhausted sometimes there was a pouring out the Lord was doing through me and it was happening on the increase with my husband on the job as well. Little did we both know that he was getting us ready because we was sharing the gospel and we was like David on the back side of the mountain he kill a bear wolf etc. And we had to allow God to kill the wolf and the bear in us. I think truly what got us here is that through all the hell we been through and hell we put others through we was truthful to the Lord and we accept accountability when he show us our ugly ways and actions. That is what got us here. We wanted to be help and fixed, we truly did but we both battle with anger and selfishness and those to spirits held us back and down. And surprisingly God put us both together that we suffer the same crisis in life and battle with the same character issues and children issues. We had severe issue in fear we both did and God made it so that we had to depend on each other in so many ways one had the lock and the other had the chain and God himself had the key! Wow this thing is true God want us to be concern about one another and to be compassion that our brother and sisters on earth get bless and filled and all be made whole that is Gods desire for us all.

Amazing grace how sweet the sounds that save a wretch like me. Looking back over my life I can really truly say God gave me a testimony! You know people God will make your life an already written song. I can sing my life song through the next chapters of this book if I wanted to. My life is consumed of how I can meet the needs of others. Consuming Fire Jesus is truly to me because my life is consume with less of me Lord and more of you through me so I can reach others by your Word and touch Lord please love through me for others can see and come to the place where you have me in you! I cannot hardly pray a prayer without me saying Father if you did for me or do it for me Lord and them every one of my brothers and sisters on planet earth. I discover that I am only bless when other share in it in some form or fashion. Lord I love what you are to me and what you is doing in our children life today. Because I realize that God is doing a universal thing for his children. I never thought that I would have a testimony that I would or could rest in God's plan of salvation for me and to your readers who might not understand the word salvation I just define it as His will and plan of blessing for us mankind. The deacon at my church say to me recently and I may have mentioned it already in these writings but he said that Liz why worry God, He always do the right thing! And I tell you people, pause and think about that statement. God doing the right thing always tells me Liz what am I worrying for if God always does the right thing. Why? Am I freighted of the decision God makes for me or on my behalf? Will He not make the right choice for me besides He is God and Lord of and over my life, He created me I am his make and model. What in the world have I been worrying for it did not forward things in my life or make things better but only cause sickness and pain and because of his grace and truth He had mercy on me and healed me every time and delivered me out of many distress in my life time and then he did what He promise He would do in his Word and delivered me from the many afflictions. So his promises are so true and He people are so faithful. So now I must tell the world that Jesus saves heals and delivers today right now this moment right here in this time He helps his people and stick with them. Please do not let anyone tell you that they are not sure that he does those things that are written in the bible. People would often say that was for then but not for now. Most people that will challenge you in your belief are a self righteous Christian. That is where in my life most of my challenges came from. Most people who have not heard the gospel will be intrigue by your sharing the gospel not challenging. Those that are new to the Christian life have mountain faith but those who have been in a while sometime will have valley faith. I am because of the Holy Spirit is challenging all concerning the written word of God concerning raising the dead and healing all manner of disease and sickness. I know that the word will be tried and tested concerning times in our life But I choose to believe the bible it plainly and clearly said that we shall raise the dead and what is beyond being dead? life? I said Lord this is written that we shall raise the dead. So if we can do this through Christ what in the world are we worry about. Because our situation is not final God's word is final A spoken word of God will raise the dead out of the grave and when that person arise they will take on a new life because the old man would have been buried and that is what God may want to do in our life is bury the old man so he could give us a new life by the spoken word over and in our life. Please audience I cannot let this subject go. Raise the dead that could be any situation or circumstances in one life. We can resurrect it with the alive and living and transforming word of God! So my spirit is shouting within me He's alive He's alive! The power in the Word and He is the Word come alive in strength and power and Glory and majesty. Let this not be just a salutation just for the hearing but let this be a salutation for the believing the promises of every word that proceed from the mouth of God which is His written Word and He became the Word made flesh. He is the spoken Word in Spirit form. You cannot see a word because it is breath, air wind. It is form and substance because you can feel it but you cannot see it or view it. But you can hear it because it is sound and energy and you also can write it to describe it or give an inscription of what you heard or trying to express. Well the word can create itself a body to dwell in and occupy a body made by it to become the description heard and felt of it. And we know that all things that were created were created by him which is and was the Word of God. So this is what I am saying that when we speak the word particular his word meaning the words that are written in the bible and agree with them, and He also will endorse our words that we say that will line up with his will. Those words spoken by us will become flesh to our personal lives and take on energy which means power which in turn power means the Holy Spirit. Then we are shown the results of the spoken words and which have been assign to the situation and circumstances. When I look back over my life and I think things over I can truly say that I been bless I have a testimony oh excuse me but his songs keeps arising on the inside of me. Looking back when I was a small child no more than two or three years old I remember how my mom and aunt was at the beach and it was so many children on the outing and my mom and aunt would drink often times on their outings and I remember going into the water and going under and hearing them in panic calling my name and under I went and suddenly they found me with panic and got the water from my lungs. I will never forget that and not long after I drank a very large quantity of bleach and the fire department came and saturated me with milk and all waited for my recovery which happen supernaturally and still not the age of five. My mother told me that at my birth my eyes were shut over a month or more and they were concern if I would have my sight. But glory to God my eyes open and I had good vision then later as a child bottle hot sauce were poured into both of my eyes attacking me with great pain. Then countless times my siblings the boys would throw me and toss in the air swinging me so dangerously if only I could describe the torment I experience it was only by the grace of God I did not have a heart attack. Later living in a home that had to be rush out do to the house being on fire. Our lives were spare three times as small children. Then 6 car accidents each time I was seriously and severely hurt the car impact was always on my side only one time I was the driver and that time it was an un license drunk driver with no brakes, driving the largest truck towing and it hit me. God allow me to survive 6 accidents. Four times guns once at parents house only 9 at the time brothers were in trouble and our house got shot up with bullets the second time I was leaving a Wednesday night bible study on a group ten day fast with church and armed men with mask held me down with gun to my head because I tried to run but they caught me and took my belongings the third time I was leaving work and two young men walk pass me and then turn around and pull out a gun and robbed me and other that was leaving the job as well and then last gun encounter I was laying on the floor in my upstairs flat and a bullet came through my window and went under my leg and lodged into the wall. Yes he is so faithful he is Jehovah Nissi my shield and banner he kept the bullets from killing me... Then the attack of the body with sickness in and out hospital so many times then I had what would be a simple surgery procedure to have my gull bladder remove little did I know that I was use as an experiment with studies and was operated on by firs time intern students which led me in intensive care and on breathing machine and family by my bed side I was cut from the top to the bottom of my torso. The hospital did not have permission at all to perform with students I met the doctor that should have done and was suppose to do the surgery. And I will finalize it with the Russian German shephards that when standing up was so large and huge that they bit me everywhere on my entire body that they could I had to be immunized I could not walk. They appearance was like lions they fur built in all. I shared this and really there is so much more but writing this book I am in amazement how the Lord have kept me alive and have me speaking and writing about Him and my journey with him. I can remember back in 1965 or66 I would say in my heart and sometimes to myself I want my father to be the biggest and strongest father ever I do not want anyone to be able to whip him I was so concern about my father being the strongest and mightiest of all the dads that I was reminded by the Holy Spirit what I said when I was a child showing that my words would manifest and come to life and he would receive me as his child and he would be that father that as a child prayed for. You see audience the devil is evil so does not fight fair. I had said those saying because every night I would have nightmare after nightmare. I can remember countless nights my mom waking me up as a small child because I would have dreams of lions and tigers and bears being in a jungle and they chasing me and I trying to climb trees to get away reaping with fear I know I had many others but this one I had over and over again until my legs would be twisted and I would have cramps and pain and be awaken my body would often be in a pretzel form. People that were so ugly the devil will take a child out in the womb of his mother. He is heartless that I am so glad that God choose us and we accepted him because he said many are the afflictions but I God shall deliver you out of them all. Mighty is our God Mighty is our God! Jeremiah said he knew us when we were yet a substance in our mother's womb. I am not ready to lie my life down in the battle there. I desire to meet the Lord in the air according the book of Thessolians. God word say it death and life is in the power of the tongue. So I hope me sharing my story was a blessing to you and a good read. I will continue my writings on stories I will like to share that are just as interest as mines. God bless and Amen Father for this writings.

www.ingramcontent.com/pod-product-compliance
Lightning Source LLC
Chambersburg PA
CBHW071322030726
47594CB00002B/509